"Your spirit is the true shield."
- Morihei Ueshiba
Aikido Founder

Copyright © Michael Jacyna

All rights reserved. No part of this publication may be reproduced or used in any way or means, electronic or mechanical, including photocopying and recording without prior written permission from the author.

For further information on this and other aikido related books visit:
ExploreAikido.com

ISBN-13: 978-1948038003
Library of Congress Control Number: 2017916277

Explore AIKIDO vol. 1

Aiki-Tai Jutsu Unarmed Techniques in Aikido

Michael Jacyna

Content

Part One · Miscellaneous

Preface 7

Aikido etiquette 8

Warm up 12

Ukemi 24

Technical division & elements 38

Tai sabaki & ashi sabaki 44

Atemi 50

Attacks in aikido 56

Technique examples 60

Part Two · Aikido Techniques

Suwari waza

    Kihon 66

    Katate tori aihanmi 74

    Katate tori gyakuhanmi 82

    Shomen uchi 86

    Ryote dori 95

Part Two · Aikido Techniques · continued

Hanmi handachi

- Katate tori gyakuhanmi 98
- Katate tori aihanmi 106
- Ryote dori 107
- Ushiro ryote dori 114
- Ushiro ryo kata dori 117

Tachi waza

- Katate tori aihanmi 118
- Katate tori gyakuhanmi 142
- Katate ryote dori 156
- Ryote dori 176
- Mune dori 194
- Ryo mune dori 208
- Kata tori men uchi 216
- Shomen uchi 230
- Yokomen uchi 246
- Tsuki 266
- Mae geri 276
- Ushiro ryote dori 286
- Katate ushiro kubi shime, Ushiro ryo kata dori, Ushiro kubi shime 302

Futari dori 316

Randori 340

Kaeshi waza 348

Glossary 397

Preface

Aikido is budo, a traditional Japanese martial art, rooted in the warrior traditions of feudal Japan. In today's society, aikido training is approached with emphasis on both the psycho-physical and spiritual development of an individual.

In this volume, I strive to present unarmed aikido techniques from an accessible and transparent viewpoint, where the reader can observe and relate to the technical aspects of the art form. Keep in mind, however, that as transparent and visually accessible this volume may be, it is not a substitute for training in the dojo under the guidance of a qualified and knowledgeable teacher who can present, explain, and clarify the nuances of each technique.

For those who have yet to experience aikido, I hope this book will inspire and ignite your journey. For aikido enthusiasts, I hope this book will serve as a fundamental guide. As for seasoned aikidokas, I hope this book will provide you with thought provoking material.

I would like to express my gratitude and appreciation to my instructors who have influenced me both on and off the mat: Jacek Wysocki, and the late Giampietro Savegnago, thank you.

I would like to thank Shirzad Alborzi for sharing his karate skills for this project. I'd also like to thank my students: Aaron Bush, Marie Visisombat, Zachary Nikolayev, and Andrey Yevdoshchenko, for their time, effort, and dedication during the photo-shoots, and the making of this book.

Aikido Etiquette

Code of conduct is an integral part of most traditional martial arts and aikido is not an exception: it begins and ends with etiquette. In fact, it is the first and easiest step to begin your budo journey.

Etiquette is an internal discipline. Complementary to our external/physical aikido curriculum, it is the practice of self-control, respect, and benevolence. Through sincere etiquette, one creates necessary channels for direct knowledge transfer from sensei (teacher) to deshi (student).

The moment we enter the dojo, we bow in tachi rei (standing bow) toward the kamiza, or to the center of the training hall. Once we step on the mat and are ready to train, we bow in za rei (seated bow).

At the beginning and end of each class, students line up facing the shomen wall. The highest ranking students sit on the right side of the line, the lower ranking adepts sit on the left side of the line, and the sensei sits in between the kamiza and the students. Before the session's bow-in and bow-out, sensei and deshi exercise mokuso (meditation). After mokuso, there is a group bow toward kamiza, followed by another bow between teacher and students. During opening and closing bow, the teacher rises up first from the bow, followed by the highest ranking student, and so on. The newest group member is the last to rise from the bow.

Line up and mokuso at the beginning and end of a class

After the class, one of the students-- usually a senior student-- offers to fold sensei's hakama. Newer or junior students offer to fold hakama for the more senior members. This custom creates mutual respect and appreciation for the time spent training together.

Some organizations may follow slight variations of the code of conduct. But overall, in most aikido dojos, you will find similar protocol implemented into the curriculum. Etiquette should not be imposed. It should be observed and naturally adopted from more advanced students and exercised by new members as they progress on their aikido path.

The following pages show bows that are commonly used during aikido training.

Bow between teacher and student

This bow exchange is done before and after the student assists the teacher in presenting techniques during the class. It is also exchanged when sensei gives the deshi feedback and/or corrections during a training session.

Za rei - Seated bow between peers

This bow is done before and after training, when students pair up to train techniques presented by the instructor. Regardless if the technique is tachi waza (standing techniques), hanmi handachi waza (seated/standing techniques), or suwari waza (seated techniques).

Tachi rei - Standing bow between peers

Students usually exercise tachi rei during tachi waza training when switching between tori (the thrower) and uke (the receiver) roles.

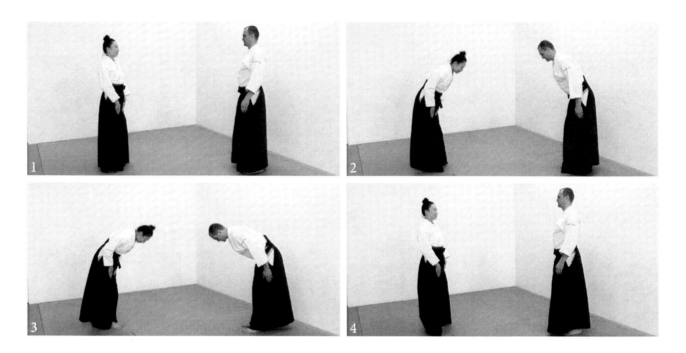

Responsibilities and attitude toward training

There is sensei and there is deshi. Each have their share of responsibilities to fulfill. Sensei's responsibility is to guide; deshi's responsibility is to follow. In most cases, it is the deshi's own choice to join a dojo to train and study. In return, it is the deshi's responsibility to tune in, observe, listen, and absorb what is given to him/her.

There are two kinds of students. The first is soto deshi (outside students). These are usually new members of the dojo, students who approach their training as a hobby, or those who can't commit to training on a regular basis. The second group of students are uchi deshi (inside students). Uchi deshi students make time for their training and their sensei. Aikido is their priority.

To become a true uchi deshi takes time, sweat, effort, and in many cases, discouragement from the sensei. It is the deshi's sole responsibility to prove their engagement and worthiness of becoming an uchi deshi. If sensei decides to take one as uchi deshi, it usually happens silently. Without a spoken word, the action will resonate loudly. Then, the true journey will begin.

Aikido Warm Up

Aikido warm-ups begin with the following exercises: shin kokyu, funakogi, and furi tama. These exercises are done in combination at the beginning of the class. The purpose of these exercises is to harmonize one's body, mind, and to unite all participants in the class.

The first part is shin kokyu, which can be loosely translated as, "spirit breath". With this exercise, we strive for a calmer state of mind, body, and unification of ki energy.

Begin in a square standing position as shown on pic. 1. Loosely place your palms together, pointing toward the ground (pic. 2). Raise your arms until your palms point toward the sky (pic. 3). Lower your arms so that your palms are at your abdominal level and pointing forward (pic. 4). Place your left palm over the right so your fingers are overlapping and your thumbs touching (pic. 5). Meditate in this position for a few moments, then raise your arms to shoulder level, and clap four times (pic. 6-8).

During shin kokyu, pointing your palms toward ground, sky, and forward, symbolizes earth, heaven, and human being, living in between. The four claps represent the unification of four elements - earth, fire, water, and wind.

Explore Aikido Vol. 1

The second exercise is funakogi, a rowing exercise. It consists of three sequences, each with different rhythm, sound, and profile stand.

The first rowing begins with the left foot in front (pic. 1-5). Hips initiate the movement with loose arms following naturally forward (pic. 1-3). On the way back, hips return first. Arms follow and end with loosely closed fists on the hips (pic. 3-5). This funakogi is done in a slow rhythm with accompanying Heii-Hoo sound. Heii being used while going forward, Hoo while moving back.

The second funakogi is performed in a right profile. Same as before, hips initiate the movement and arms follow. It is performed faster than the first one and the accompanying sound is Heii-Heii.

The third funakogi is in a left profile. Hips initiate the movement. Arms with closed fists swiftly follow downward (pic. 1-3). On the way back, release your fists and return to your hips. This is the fastest of the three funakogi exercises. The accompanying sound is Heii-Tsaa.

The third exercise is furi tama. It can be interpreted as, "the vibration of the soul". It is the element inserted after each funakogi, shown on the previous page.

After each funakogi sequence, shift from profile position to square stance (pic. 1). Place your palms together and point forward (pic. 2). Fold your palms left over right (pic. 3-5). Once in this position, shake the grip up and down (pic. 6-7).

During furi tama, breathe in through the nose and exhale through the mouth. Your posture should be upright with spine vertically aligned. As you vibrate the grip, your body should relax so that the grip vibration can transfer throughout the spine, from sacrum to cervical.

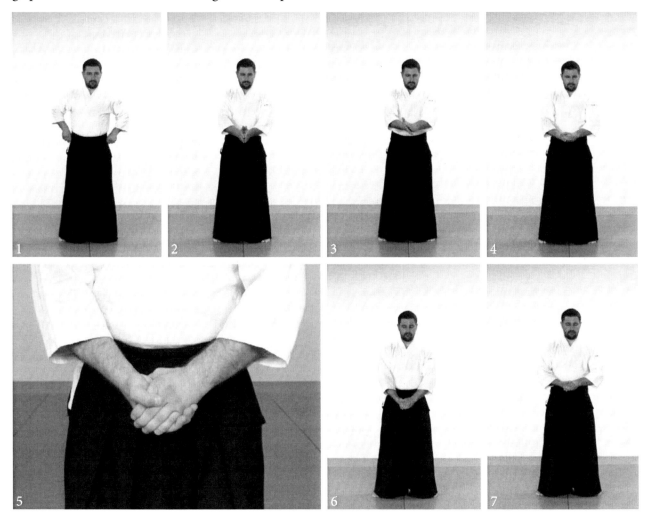

Here is the order of the full set of shin kokyu, funakogi, and furi tama performed together:

1. Shin kokyu, 2. Funakogi in left profile, 3. Furi tama, 4. Funakogi in right profile, 5. Furi tama, 6. Funakogi in left profile, 7. Furi tama, 8. This whole set ends with shin kokyu, which varies slightly from the one performed at the beginning. It is shown and explained on page 16.

After the last furi tama, perform the final shin kokyu. Clap four times (pic. 1-2). Point your palms toward earth and heaven (pic. 3-4). Rise to your toes and lock your palms interlocking fingers and thumbs inward. Swiftly bring the hold to abdominal level with accompanying Heii sound (pic. 5-7). As you inhale, open the grip and release accumulated energy with arms spreading wide open (pic. 8-9). As you exhale, close your arms and bring your palms toward your abdomen (pic. 10). Repeat inhale and exhale three times. Finish this exercise by raising your arms with palms open and shake off remaining tension (pic. 11-12).

Explore Aikido Vol. 1

Sayo undo and mune hineri is another set of aikido warm up exercises. Both are a good way to work on meguri (rotational movements of your forearms) and gain understanding of the importance of hips work in aikido.

1. Sayo undo is an exercise in seiza, with knees wide spread. Begin by placing your palms with thumbs up, onto your thighs (pic. 1). Lean left and right and simultaneously rotate your forearms as you drop side to side. It is important that the arm rotation begins with the hip motion.

2. Mune hineri is another aikido warm up exercise in seiza. Loosely place your palms on your thighs (pic. 1). Start by moving forward your left hip, torso, and left shoulder. Your left arm follows with simultaneous rotation of your forearm. At the end of the rotation, your thumb is pointing down, and your right hand is pulled back, palm up, next to your right hip (pic. 2). Alternate left and right side (pic. 3).

3. Kokyu stretch follows after the two previous exercises. Start in seiza with palms on your thighs (pic. 1). Inhale as you raise your arms (pic. 2-3). Once your arms are up, close your palms, exhale, and lower your arms with elbows leading. End with arms stretched forward and palms by your thighs (pic. 4-6).

Neck warm up. The following exercises are self explanatory, see below:

1. Back and forth head movement.

2. Side to side head movement.

3. Shoulder to shoulder head tilt.

4. Head rotation in both left and right directions.

5. Look up and shake. Tilt your head back and shake left and right. Relax your jaw and facial muscles.

Wrist stretching exercises are done on both arms. All wrist stretches should be done with moderation and within the limits of one's pain threshold.

1. Nikyo - stretch your left arm forward, thumb down. Squeeze your left palm's pinky and thumb. Bring the hold toward your center, then move slightly lower (pic. 1-4). The overall trajectory is a vertical, elliptical motion.

2. Sankyo - position your left forearm facing palm down, forward and elbow pointing up. With your right hand, hold your left wrist and torque the forearm inward while simultaneously moving it sideways and up (pic. 1-4). The overall trajectory of sankyo is a diagonal, elliptical motion.

3. Kotegaeshi - position your left palm pointing up, facing toward you, and elbow pointing down. With your right fingers, hold your left thumb abductor muscle. With your right thumb, press on the back of your left hand. Rotate your left wrist toward the outside (pic. 1-4).

4. Nikyo-yonkyo - With your right hand, hold your left wrist. Bring the grip up until you feel tension in your left wrist (pic. 1-2). Stretch the grip forward. With the base of your right index finger, apply pressure to your left forearm, just above the wrist (pic. 3-4).

Legs warm up and stretch.

1. Knee stretch. Stand with one leg forward and lean on your knee with your upper body weight. Stretch both left and right knee.

2. Low squad stretch left and right. Start with one leg in a deep squat position and the other leg stretched out, then switch to the other side. During the transition to the other side, try to keep your hips as low as possible to the ground as it makes the exercise more challenging.

3. Knees circle. Place your feet together, bend your knees, and hold them with your hands. Begin knee circles in left and then right direction.

Explore Aikido Vol. 1

4. Reaching forward. Sit upright with legs together and stretched forward. Reach your toes and hold. If you are unable to reach your toes, try reaching your ankles.

5. Split forward, left and right. Spread your legs and lean all the way forward or until you feel the stretch. After you reach your left toes and pull forward, reach your right toes and pull forward.

6. Butterfly. After the split, bring your feet together. Hold both of your big toes with your right hand while your left hand holds the remaining toes (pic. 1). In this position, move your knees up and down (pic. 2-4).

7. Knees side to side. After the above exercises, bring your knees up and your feet together. Move your knees left to right. This is a good exercise to release tension after leg warm up stretching.

Rocking. The following set of back and forth rocking exercises is a good way to warm up and stretch your back, legs, and strengthen your core. Rocking is incorporated into most aikido warm ups before rolling and falling.

1. First set begins with legs stretched forward. As you rock back, your arms follow all the way back to the mat. At that point, swiftly touch your palms with your toes, then rock back to seated position with legs forward. Once upright, reach your toes and stretch.

2. Second set begins in a seated profile position with left leg in front. Push left leg off the mat and go up and back. Your right leg follows and "switches" with the left leg. The momentum created will bring you back to seated position. Finish with the right leg in front. Note that legs alternation happens as you rock back, and after each rocking you end up with the opposite leg in front.

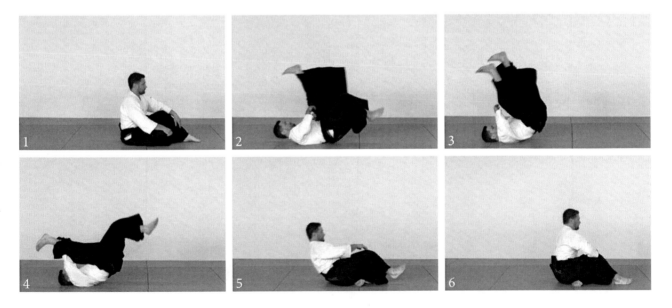

Explore Aikido Vol. 1

3. Third set begins in a half position, with left leg in front. The dorsal of your right foot, including toes, is flat on the mat. From this position, slide into rocking. Repeat the sequence as in the previous seated rocking exercise. On the way back, it is necessary to place your left foot dorsal flat on the mat. Finish in half position, right leg in front.

4. Fourth set of the rocking exercises begins in a standing position, left leg in front. Slide from standing into rocking by placing your right foot dorsal flat on the mat, and rock back. Switch legs and finish with right foot in front. The rockings are usually done 10 times of each set, for a total of 40.

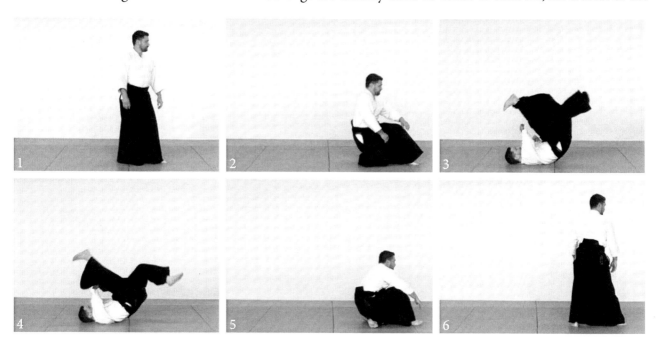

Ukemi

Ukemi, the art of rolling and falling in aikido, is a very important part of our training. The main role of ukemi is injury prevention through safe escape from aikido techniques. During aikido sessions, students usually train in pairs. One of the students is tori; the other is uke. Uke receives the technique and most of the time ends up in some sort of ukemi. On the following pages, you can see a few useful ukemi examples.

1. Suwari ushiro ukemi is a seated back roll. Start in a seated position with one foot in front and the other foot folded beneath. Push the front foot off the ground and above your right shoulder. This creates momentum for the roll. Your head should be tilted toward the left knee to make space for your shoulder to roll over the mat. At the end you will finish in seiza.

2. Ushiro ukemi is a back roll from the half position. It is often trained after warm up and before the actual training session. Begin in a half position, rock back, and roll over your shoulder. Finish in a half position with the opposite leg in front. For example, if you start with right foot in front you should finish with left foot in front.

3. Ushiro ukemi, back roll from a standing position. Start in a profile stance with one foot in front. Slide into a seated position and roll back. Try to keep your "touch down" foot (pic. 5) as close to your body as you can, as it is easier to stand from the roll.

4. Suwari zenpo kaiten ukemi is a seated forward roll. Start in seiza with one knee forward and one knee sideways (pic. 1). Lean in and roll forward over your left arm and shoulder. Your right hand can act as a support (pic. 2-3). Finish the roll in seiza (pic. 6), or in a seated position with one knee up (pic. 6b).

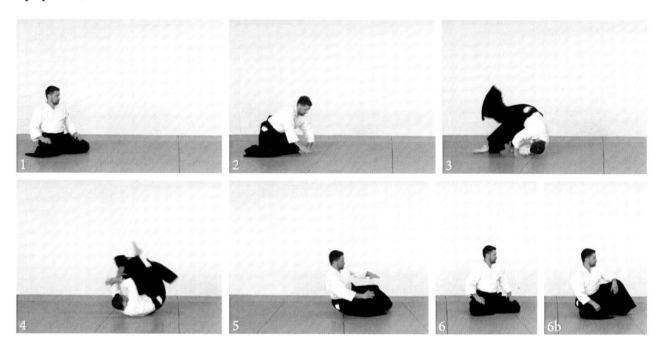

5. Zenpo kaiten ukemi- forward roll from the half position. Start in a half seated position. Lean in, push off the ground with your right leg, and slide into the roll. Remember to roll over the same arm as to whichever leg is in front. For example: if your left leg is in front, roll over your left arm. If your right leg is in front, roll over your right arm.

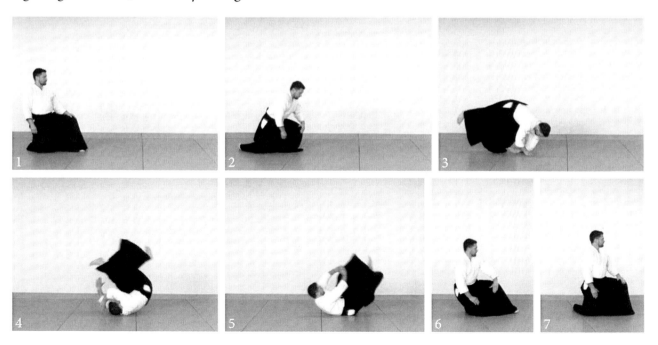

6. Zenpo kaiten ukemi, forward roll from standing position. Start with your left leg in front, and roll over your left arm and shoulder. Finish in a standing position with left leg in front.

Zenpo kaiten ukemi and ushiro ukemi are the basic aikido rolls. Both incorporate elements of rocking exercises shown in the warm up chapter.

Explore Aikido Vol. 1

7. Break fall, as the name suggests, is a roll with a "break". Begin zenpo kaiten ukemi in left profile. To slow down, hit the mat with your right hand (pic. 4). Instead of getting up, unfold your legs and finish the fall on the ground (pic. 6).

8. Kote ukemi, is basically a break fall in mid air. It is used in many aikido techniques such as kotegaeshi, sumi otoshi, kokyu nage, and sudori nage, just to name a few.

9. **Fish fall** is a fall where your upper body falls first, followed by your lower body and legs. The overall movement of fish ukemi is backward. Seated fish fall is usually incorporated into the warm up. Things to remember during this fall is: when looking to the right, use your right leg to kick back (pic. 3). If you look to the left, use your left leg. This is less strenuous and your body will be properly aligned.

Explore Aikido Vol. 1

10. Fish fall from a standing position (pic. 1-8). Fish fall is incorporated mainly into ikkyo, nikyo, sankyo, yonkyo, and gokyo techniques.

12. Free fall aka irimi ukemi (pic. 1-10). This fall is important during irimi nage, yoko irimi, tenchi nage, aiki otoshi, shiho nage sankyo, and other techniques.

11. Free fall in slow motion. Begin in a wide squat position. Look over your right shoulder. On a big, circular, vertical trajectory, reach back with your right arm. During your palm touch down with tatami, make sure to have a visual contact. This helps to position your body for the fall (pic. 1-4). While pushing your hips up, slide from your palm to your right and then left shoulder (pic. 5). Kick both legs up and forward.

13. Kote ukemi #1. Hold your training partner's hand as shown in pic. 1. Lean forward and slide into the fall. Your free hand should hit the mat before your body (pic. 5). This will absorb the impact of the fall and results in a softer fall.

14. Kote ukemi #2. Another way to train kote ukemi is over a kneeling partner. Wrap your arm around your partner's torso and slide into the fall. Your free hand should be first to hit the mat.

15. Koshi ukemi, hip fall. Your partner holds your wrist, squats down, and loads you onto his lower back (pic. 1-4). At this point, wrap your other arm around his shoulder or hold onto his uniform's lapel (pic. 5, 5b). Once you hold on, your partner will rise and slide you off his hips (pic. 6-8).

16. Irimi ukemi, free fall with a partner #1. Your partner stands with arms spread sideways (pic. 1). Approach one of his arms and wrap your arm around his (pic. 2-3). Let your legs fly forward (pic. 4-6). Your palm or forearm will touch the mat first (pic. 7-8).

17. Irimi ukemi, free fall with a partner #2. This example is the same as above, except you don't wrap your hand around your partner's arm.

Technical Divisions & Elements

Technical divisions and elements in aikido. There are several divisions in aikido. Clarifying them makes it easier to study, understand, and progress in aikido training.

1. Aiki-tai jutsu - unarmed aikido techniques are trained in three different positions:
A) seated, B) seated/standing and C) standing.

A) Suwari waza - seated position techniques are trained in seiza.

B) Hanmi handachi waza - techniques where tori is seated and uke is standing.

C) Tachi waza - techniques trained in a standing position. The most popular of the three training options.

2. Omote and Ura

A) Omote concept - omote techniques are based on centripetal force. They use irmi entry movement and immediate center line control. They tend to be direct and shorter in nature than ura techniques. In most omote forms, we execute techniques in "front" of the uke.

Omote technique example:
Irimi Nage Omote (pic. 1-5).

B) Ura concept - ura techniques are based on centrifugal force. Ura techniques redirect uke's energy, with a pivot for example, and in most cases are executed "behind" the uke.

Ura technique example:
Irimi Nage Ura (pic. 1-5).

Note that many techniques have elements of both omote and ura. Therefore, they are difficult to categorize as strictly omote or ura.

3. Osae and Nage

A) Osae are pinning techniques based on joint locking and immobilization. Ikkyo, nikyo, sankyo, yonkyo, and gokyo, to name a few, may be categorized into osae group.

Osae technique example:
Ude Kime Osae (pic. 1-5).

B) Nage are throwing techniques. Irimi nage, yoko irimi, sumi otoshi, tenchi nage, and kaiten nage, are a few techniques in the nage group.

Nage technique example:
Ude Kime Nage (pic. 1-5).

4. Distance

In aiki-tai jutsu, we work in three distances:

A) Chikama is a short distance between tori and uke. It is usually applied in suwari waza. It is a distance where the other person is within arms reach, without having to take any steps. This distance is favorable to uke as it leaves little reaction time for tori.

B) Itto no maai is a natural distance in which tori and uke are one step away. It is the most common distance applied during tachi waza training, as it provides healthy amount of time for uke to attack and enough time for tori to react.

C) Toma is a long distance where tori and uke are two steps away. This distance is favorable to tori as it gives more reaction time and less favorable to uke as it takes longer to reach tori and execute desired attack. Usually, toma distance is applied during kokyu nage techniques where we need solid amount of kinetic energy. Toma distance is also applied within aiki-jo, and aiki-ken training.

5. Timing

Timing is a very important element in aikido training. There are three distinctive timing options:

A) Go no sen is a reactive timing. It is a timing where tori reacts to uke's actions. Tori basically waits until uke attacks and then reacts. It is a basic timing application.

B) Sen no sen is simultaneous timing. In this case, both uke and tori begin their action at the same time. It is intermediate level timing.

C) Sen sen no sen is preemptive timing. It is the most difficult timing of the three options. It is a timing where tori begins defense before uke physically starts attack. It almost seems as uke/tori roles were reversed. This is advanced timing.

6. Apply technique on yourself

In order to properly set up and execute aikido techniques, in many cases, we first have to apply a technique on ourself. In order to do that we would offer our hand to uke in a certain position (nikyo, sankyo, kotegaeshi, etc.). It is a concept that needs to be presented and transmitted from teacher to student in person in order to fully grasp it.

7. Meguri

Meguri are rotational movements of the forearms. Meguri are incorporated into all aikido repertoire. Their purpose is to maximize technical efficiency. Note that meguri begins with hips movement, which is then transferred to the forearms. Meguri are partially responsible for acceleration- speeding up uke, absorption- drawing uke into the technique, and kuzushi- placing uke into an off balance position.

8. Acceleration

Accelerating, or speeding up uke, is especially valuable when some techniques require a lot of kinetic energy. Acceleration is usually achieved by changing the distance between uke and tori and meguri movements.

9. Absorption

Absorption, or drawing uke in, should be incorporated into all aspects of aikido training. Absorption may be achieved by meguri, a temporary distance change between tori and uke, or body repositioning within the same distance. In some instances, it can be achieved by doing nothing and just waiting. Regardless of how you achieve the element of drawing uke in, it should always be part of aikido training. Even when absorption is not visible to the eye, it should still be present.

10. Kuzushi

Kuzushi means an off balance position. It is a very important element that needs to be incorporated into all throwing techniques. Without kuzushi, it is difficult to throw someone. Kuzushi may be achieved by meguri, distance change between tori and uke, and atemi application (see page 50).

Please note that timing, meguri, acceleration, absorption, and kuzushi are incorporated into the techniques simultaneously, and are more or less interdependent.

Tai Sabaki & Ashi Sabaki

Tai sabaki and ashi sabaki are body movements and foot work that refer to specific aikido techniques. They are used to move off the line of the oncoming attack, and/or to create free passage for uke to pass by. There are a few tai sabaki and ashi sabaki that are incorporated into everyday aikido training, and are therefore necessary to be familiar with.

1. Tenkan is a 180° pivot. Most of the time, we pivot on the front foot. See below, side, and front view of tenkan tai sabaki.

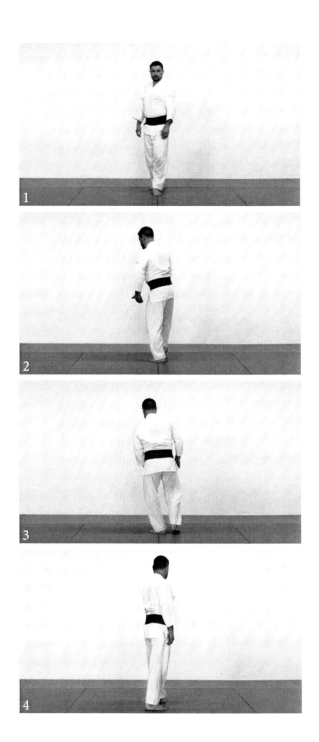

2. **Irimi Tenkan** is a step forward (ayumi ashi omote) and a pivot (tenkan). The movement begins with the head and the rest of the body follows.

3. 270° irimi is a rotational body movement, where we pivot forward on the front foot.

4. Ayumi ashi are steps forward or back. These are the natural alternating steps we take while walking. See examples below:

Ayumi ashi omote

Ayumi ashi ura

5. Tsugi ashi are shuffle steps. These steps are used often during training, doing both omote- forward and ura- back tsugi ashi steps. See examples below:

Tsugi ashi omote

Tsugi ashi ura

Atemi

Atemi are strikes. Essential elements within aikido repertoire, they are applied through punches or kicks. There are two kinds of atemi. The first group is "filler" atemi. These are strikes incorporated within aikido technique and are partially responsible for setting up the desired technique. The second group are "finishing" or "application" atemi. As the name suggests, the purpose of these strikes is to end the encounter with the opponent right at the beginning. On the following pages are examples of filler and application atemi.

1. Nikyo irimi technique.

Atemi application for nikyo irimi.

2. Yoko irimi technique.

Atemi application for yoko irimi.

3. Filler atemi example within kaiten nage technique from shomen uchi attack (pic. 3 & 5).

4. Filler atemi example within irimi nage technique from yokomen uchi attack (pic. 2, 4, 5).

5. Atemi and target areas examples.

Temple

Nose

Face/head elbow atemi

Ribs

Head knee atemi

Groin

Chin

Double atemi

Chin/face

Attacks in Aikido

In order to train aikido in a progressive manner, it is necessary to have a training partner who is able to execute proper attack. This means beginning the attack from a proper distance, projecting a sufficient amount of energy, and finishing the attack in a correct position/stance. Attacks in aikido are comprised of grips, strikes, and kicks. In some cases, the grip attacks are combined with a strike or punch. Remember, without a proper attack and commitment it can be fatiguing to apply techniques. Before jumping into more advance training, aikidokas should be familiar with the following attacks:

Katate tori aihanmi - cross grip

Katate tori gyakuhanmi - mirrored grip

Katate ryote dori - two hands one hand grip

Ryote dori - two hands two hands grip

Ryo mune dori - two hands chest grip

Kata dori men uchi - shoulder grip combined with shomen uchi strike

Shomen uchi - direct strike to the head, from top down

Yokomen uchi - side strike to the head

The following attacks are ushiro tori, ending in the back. Keep in mind for training purposes all ushiro dori attacks begin in front and end in the back, behind tori.

Ushiro ryote dori - two hands grip from the back

Ushiro ryo kata dori - two hands shoulder grip from the back

Ushiro katate kubishime - one hand grip combined with a choke from the back

Ushiro kubishime - choke from the back

Ushiro tori - "bear hug" from the back

Judan tsuki - direct punch to the body

Jodan tsuki - direct punch to the head

Mae geri - front kick

Yoko geri - side kick

Mawashi geri - round house kick to the head

Ura mawashi geri - reverse roundhouse kick

Aikido Technique Examples

There are a variety of techniques in aikido repertoire. The following pictures present singular techniques during their most typical moment. Besides the mechanical aspect of each technique, there are many additional factors to successfully execute them. These are outlined in the technical divisions and elements chapter. Please remember there is no substitute for a skilled and knowledgeable teacher who can present and explain the techniques in person.

Ikkyo - is done through uke's arm control

Nikyo - is done through wrist lock application. Uke's arm should be in "s" shape position

Sankyo - third technique is done through wrist, elbow, and shoulder lock application

Yonkyo - is done through pressure point application on the forearm

Gokyo - this particular gokyo (pic. 5), is done through simultaneous combination of five movements. Pic. 6 shows a more commonly known gokyo technique.

Kotegaeshi - technique done through wrist lock, can be performed as a throw or pin

Shiho nage - four direction throw, can be applied with or with out joint locking

Irimi nage - entry throw

Yoko irimi - side entry throw

Sumi otoshi - corner drop technique, executed through wrist and elbow control

Tai otoshi - body drop technique, is done though wrist control and entry under uke's armpit

Explore Aikido Vol. 1

Ude kime nage - throw technique is done through arm/elbow pressure

Ude kime osae - pinning technique is done through arm/elbow pressure

Sudori nage - a technique where tori "dives" under uke's legs

Koshi nage - hip throw

Tenchi nage - heaven and earth technique that stretches uke's arms up and down

Juji garami - cross throw is done through wrapping over uke's arms

Kaiten nage - wheel throw. Uke's arm is used as a leverage to throw

Aiki otoshi - is a technique where we pull uke's legs forward and up

Kokyu nage - literally meaning "breath throw". There are many kokyu nage techniques, the common element to all of them is redirection of uke's energy

The following techniques are combining two techniques into one.

Nikyo irimi - combination of nikyo and irimi nage

Shiho nage irimi - combination of shiho nage and irimi nage

Shiho nage sankyo - combination of shiho nage and sankyo

Ude kime koshi nage - combination of ude kime nage and koshi nage

Kotegaeshi shiho nage #1

Kotegaeshi shiho nage #2

Combination of kotegaeshi and shiho nage

Suwari Waza

Suwari waza are seated techniques trained in seiza. Kihon are basic techniques. They are meant for studying purposes and refining the basic form. Kihon suwari waza techniques are practiced in a square position with partners facing each other, their knees almost touching. The timing applied during these kihon techniques is sen sen no sen, preemptive timing, where tori begins his technique before uke's attack. Ideally, at the moment of uke's intention to attack, if the timing is correctly applied, it almost appears as the tori/uke roles are reversed.

Suwari waza · kihon - ikkyo

Begin jodan tsuki with right hand. Uke responds with right forearm block (pic. 1-3). Steer uke's block sideways, simultaneously open your knee to the side, and finish ikkyo omote (pic. 4-6). At the end, apply ikkyo pin (pic. 7).

Suwari waza · kihon - nikyo omote

Begin jodan tsuki with right hand. Uke responds with right forearm block (pic. 1-3). Take control of uke's elbow and apply nikyo hold on uke's right hand (pic. 4-6). Finish nikyo omote (pic. 7). Apply nikyo omote pin by slightly bending uke's arm in the elbow and pressing uke's palm inward and forward (pic. 8).

Suwari waza · kihon - nikyo ura

Begin jodan tsuki with right hand. Uke responds with right forearm block (pic. 2-3). Simultaneously take control of uke's right forearm. Apply nikyo ura hold and shift back (pic. 4-5). Bring nikyo hold to your upper chest area, just under your collar bone and apply nikyo ura (pic. 6-7). In between nikyo ura and nikyo ura pin, there is a vise, a squeeze where you bring together nikyo hold and the hold behind uke's triceps (pic. 8). From the vise position, turn uke to the mat (pic. 9-10). Apply nikyo ura pin (pic. 11).

Suwari waza · kihon - sankyo

Begin jodan tsuki with right hand. Uke responds with right forearm block (pic. 2-3). With your left hand take control of uke's elbow. With your right hand, take over uke's palm (pic. 4). Elevate the palm hold with a simultaneous sankyo rotation inward (pic. 5). Take over the sankyo hold with your left hand. With a smooth cut down, bring uke to the mat and finish sankyo pin (pic. 6-8).

Explore Aikido vol. 1

Suwari waza · kihon - yonkyo

Begin jodan tsuki with right hand. Uke responds with right forearm block (pic. 2-3). With your left hand take control of uke's elbow. With your right hand, take over uke's right wrist (pic. 4). Add your left hand grip to uke's right forearm and apply yonkyo (pic. 5). Yonkyo goes through uke's center to your center. The trajectory of this technique is diagonal (pic. 6-7). Apply yonkyo pin (pic. 8).

Suwari waza · kihon - gokyo

Begin jodan tsuki with right hand. Uke responds with right forearm block (pic. 2-3). With your left hand take control of uke's elbow. With your right hand take over uke's right wrist (pic. 4). Start the gokyo application by simultaneously bringing uke's arm toward your center, then down, up, back, and forward (pic. 5-8).

Suwari waza · kihon - nanakyo

Begin jodan tsuki with right hand. Uke responds with right forearm block (pic. 2-3). With your left hand take control of uke's elbow. With your right hand take over uke's right palm/wrist. At the same time move back (pic. 5-6). Apply nanakyo by squeezing uke's palm and forearm together. Bring the hold down and forward (pic. 6-8).

The following suwari waza techniques are in a profile position.

Suwari waza · katate tori aihanmi - ikkyo omote

Offer your right hand for uke to grab (pic. 1-2). As uke connects, absorb uke in and apply ikkyo omote through uke's center line (pic. 3-8).

Suwari waza · katate tori aihanmi - ikkyo ura

Offer your right hand for uke to grab (pic. 1-2). As uke connects, simultaneously rotate back and apply ikkyo ura (pic. 3-8).

Suwari waza · katate tori aihanmi - nikyo omote

Offer your right hand, thumb down, for uke to grab (pic. 1-2). As uke connects, bring uke forward and take control of uke's elbow. With your right hand take over uke's right hand and apply nikyo hold (pic. 3-6). Finish nikyo omote by bringing the whole grip down (pic. 7-8). At the end apply nikyo omote pin (pic. 9).

Suwari waza · katate tori aihanmi - nikyo ura

Offer your right hand, thumb down, for uke to grab (pic. 1-2). Wrap your right hand around uke's wrist, with your left hand take hold of uke's grip and finish nikyo ura toward uke's center (pic. 3-6). At the end, apply nikyo ura pin (pic. 7).

Suwari waza · katate tori aihanmi - sankyo omote

Offer your right hand for uke to grab (pic. 1-2). As uke attempts to grab your wrist, take over uke's palm and rotate it to a sankyo position (pic. 3-4). Then take over uke's wrist with your left hand and finish sankyo omote with a smooth cut downward (pic. 5-7). At the end apply sankyo pin (pic. 8).

Suwari waza · katate tori aihanmi - sankyo ura

Offer your right hand for uke to grab (pic. 1). As uke attempts to grab your wrist, take over uke's palm and regrab it with your left hand (pic. 2-3). Slide your right hand to uke's elbow and simultaneously bring the sankyo hold palm to your quad (pic. 4). Throw uke back by opening your left knee sideways (pic. 5). Bring uke to the front by closing your position with left knee (pic. 6-7). At the end apply sankyo pin (pic. 8-10).

Suwari waza · katate tori aihanmi - yonkyo

Offer your right hand, thumb down, for uke to grab (pic. 1-2). As uke connects, simultaneously switch profile. With your left hand, take over uke's forearm and finish yonkyo (pic. 3-6). At the end, apply yonkyo pin (pic. 7).

Suwari waza · katate tori aihanmi - kotegaeshi

Offer your left hand, palm up, for uke to grab. As uke connects, simultaneously move back. With your right hand apply atemi and take over uke's left wrist (pic. 1-3). With your left hand apply kotegaeshi by pressing downward and outward on the backside of uke's palm (pic. 4-5). Once uke goes into the fall, slide your left hand from uke's palm to uke's elbow pit (pic. 6). Use the momentum and rotate uke into the finish pin position (pic. 8-9). Apply kotegaeshi pin (pic. 10).

Suwari waza · katate tori gyakuhanmi - nikyo ura

Offer your left hand for uke to grab. At the moment of connection, open your position by shifting left knee sideways. With your right hand apply atemi. Your left palm is open with four fingers together and thumb separate (pic. 2). This allows you to take over uke's wrist and apply nikyo ura (pic. 3-6). Finish with transitional vise and nikyo pin (pic. 7-10).

Suwari waza · katate tori gyakuhanmi - yonkyo omote

Offer your left hand for uke to grab (pic. 1). At the moment of connection your forearm is almost in a kotegaeshi position (pic. 2). With your left hand take over yonkyo grip and with your right hand apply atemi (pic. 3). Add your right hand to uke's wrist and finish yonkyo (pic. 4-8).

Suwari waza · katate tori gyakuhanmi - kotegaeshi

Offer your right hand for uke to grab (pic. 1). As uke connects, your forearm is in a nikyo position (pic. 2). From above, take over uke's wrist and execute kotegaeshi including finish pin (pic. 3-10).

Suwari waza · katate tori gyakuhanmi - kotegaeshi shiho nage

Offer your right hand for uke to grab. Once uke connects (pic. 1-2), lift the hold to eye level to loosen and create an opening in uke's grip (pic. 3). Slide your left hand into uke's grip and take over uke's palm. Remove your right hand from uke's grip and take over uke's palm from the top (pic. 4-5). Finish kotegaeshi-shiho nage by swiftly bringing the grip downward (pic. 6-8).

Suwari waza · shomen uchi - ikkyo omote

Uke begins with shomen uchi attack (pic. 1-2). Take control over uke's elbow and wrist. Move forward and execute ikkyo omote (pic. 2-8).

Suwari waza · shomen uchi - ikkyo ura

Uke begins with shomen uchi attack (pic. 1-2). Take control over uke's elbow and wrist. Simultaneously pivot back and execute ikkyo ura (pic. 3-8).

Suwari waza · shomen uchi - nikyo omote

Uke begins with shomen uchi attack (pic. 1-2). Take control over uke's elbow and push it forward. Use your right hand to take over uke's right hand and finish nikyo omote (pic. 3-10).

Suwari waza · shomen uchi - nikyo ura

Uke begins with shomen uchi attack (pic. 1-2). Take control over uke's right forearm and move back (pic. 3-4). Continue and finish nikyo ura (pic. 6-10).

Suwari waza · shomen uchi - sankyo omote

Uke begins with shomen uchi attack (pic.1-2). Take control over uke's right elbow and wrist. Push uke's arm forward so that uke ends up in kuzushi (pic. 3-4). While still holding uke's elbow, slide your right hand to uke's palm (pic. 5). With your left hand regrab sankyo hold (pic. 6). Continue and finish sankyo omote (pic. 7-10).

Suwari waza · shomen uchi - sankyo ura

Uke begins with shomen uchi attack (pic. 1). Simultaneously take control over uke's wrist and palm and move back. With your left hand take over sankyo hold (pic. 2-4). Slide your right hand to uke's elbow and bring the sankyo hold down to your quad (pic. 5). Throw uke back by opening your knee sideways (pic. 6). Close your knee and bring uke to the front (pic. 7-8). Exchange your hands on the sankyo hold and finish sankyo pin (pic. 9-10).

Suwari waza · shomen uchi - kotegaeshi

Uke begins with shomen uchi attack (pic. 1). Simultaneously take hold of uke's wrist and shift back (pic. 2-3). Pull uke forward and execute kotegaeshi (pic. 4-6). Finish kotegaeshi by rotating uke face down and apply kotegaeshi pin (pic. 7-10).

Suwari waza · shomen uchi - kaiten nage

Uke begins with shomen uchi attack (pic. 1-2). With your right arm, connect with the attack at the elbow area and let it fall down. Simultaneously move back (pic. 3-4). Once the shomen uchi is down, use your left forearm to keep control of uke's elbow. With your right hand apply atemi and take control of uke's neck (pic. 5-6). Execute kaiten nage by rotating uke's neck and right elbow forward (pic. 7-9).

Suwari waza · shomen uchi - ude kime nage

Uke begins with shomen uchi attack. With your right forearm, connect with the attack and immediately take control of uke's palm. With your left hand take control of uke's elbow and simultaneously shift back (pic. 1-4). Execute ude kime nage by pushing uke's elbow forward while holding back uke's palm (pic. 5-8).

Suwari waza · ryote dori - kokyu ho #1

Kokyu ho is trained in a square position with ryote dori grip (pic. 1). As uke is about to catch your hands, simultaneously lift your right and lower your left forearm to place uke into kuzushi (pic. 2). Bring your left arm to your left hip and with your right hand push toward uke's shoulder (pic. 3). Uke rolls to the side while still holding your wrist. As uke is on the way up to seiza, offer your right hand onto uke's center line. This will force uke to grab your hand and avoid the possibility of being hit (pic. 4-5). As uke is almost in seiza, begin meguri with your right forearm and apply kokyu ho yoko irimi (pic. 6-12).

Suwari waza · katate ryote dori - kokyu ho #2

Uke begins with ryote dori hold down (pic. 1-2). Relax your forearms and pull back your elbows (pic. 3-5). Once you bring your hands to your torso, go slightly up, push uke back, and let your arms follow forward (pic. 6-8).

Suwari waza · katate ryote dori - kokyu ho #3

Uke begins with ryote dori hold down (pic. 1-2). Begin by simultaneously closing and folding your palms inward and bringing your elbows together onto your center line. This will cause uke to go up and extend his arms (pic. 3-6). Once uke is in kuzushi, unfold your arms and push uke back (pic. 7-10).

Hanmi Handachi Waza

Hanmi handachi waza are techniques where tori is in seiza and uke attacks standing. Due to tori's limited maneuverability, it requires extra attention in incorporating sayo undo, mune hineri, and meguri elements within this form.

Hanmi handachi waza · katate tori gyakuhanmi - nikyo ura

Offer your left hand for uke to grab. As uke approaches and connects, pull your forearm onto your center line and absorb uke forward (pic. 1-3). Once uke is pulled to the front, apply judan atemi to move/push uke out (pic. 4-5). Take over uke's wrist and apply nikyo ura (pic. 6-9). Finish with nikyo vise and nikyo pin (pic. 10-12).

Hanmi handachi waza · katate tori gyakuhanmi - sankyo omote

Offer your left hand for uke to grab. As uke approaches and connects, pull your forearm onto your center line and absorb uke forward (pic. 1-3). Once uke is pulled to the front, apply judan atemi to move uke out (pic. 4-5). Take over uke's wrist, apply sankyo hold, execute sankyo omote, and finish sankyo pin (pic. 6- 12).

Hanmi handachi waza · katate tori gyakuhanmi - kotegaeshi

Offer your left hand, palm up, for uke to grab (pic. 1-2). At the moment of connection, your hand should be in a thumb down position, with the thumb being over uke's wrist. This allows you to immediately take over uke's wrist (pic. 3-4). Pull uke forward into kuzushi (pic. 5). Change the direction and execute kotegaeshi (pic. 6-11).

Hanmi handachi waza · katate tori gyakuhanmi - shiho nage

Offer your left hand for uke to grab (pic. 1-2). At the moment of connection, your hand should be in a thumb down position so that your and uke's palms are connected (pic. 3). Bring uke down toward your center. With both hands apply shiho nage hold (pic. 4). With wrist and elbow lock, bring uke behind your back and execute shiho nage (pic. 5-11).

Hanmi handachi waza · katate tori gyakuhanmi - sumi otoshi

Offer your left hand for uke to grab (pic. 1-2). At the moment of connection, absorb uke forward (pic. 3-4). Once uke is in front of you, swiftly open your left arm sideways and with your right hand enter into uke's right elbow pit (pic. 5-6). Finish sumi otoshi by pushing uke's elbow out in a big circular motion (pic. 7-11).

Hanmi handachi waza · katate tori gyakuhanmi - kokyu nage #1

Offer your left hand for uke to grab (pic. 1-2). As uke connects, bring your elbow onto your center line and absorb uke forward. Continue to pull the grip all the way to the other side (pic. 3-4). As uke passes by, apply meguri and finish kokyu nage (pic. 5-9).

Hanmi handachi waza · katate tori gyakuhanmi - kokyu nage #2

Offer your right hand for uke to grab (pic. 1-2). As uke approaches and connects, pull the hold up and forward. Simultaneously with your left hand apply atemi onto uke's center line (pic. 4-5). Bring your right hand down and with your left forearm push uke's elbow pit forward (pic. 6-11).

Hanmi handachi waza · katate tori aihanmi - sankyo omote

Offer your right hand for uke to grab. At the moment of connection, your hand should be in a sankyo position (pic. 1-2). Move back and change your profile. With left hand regrab sankyo hold (pic. 3-4). Execute sankyo by bringing the hold down (pic. 5-8). Apply sankyo pin (pic. 9-10).

Hanmi handachi waza · ryote dori - kotegaeshi

Offer both hands for uke to grab (pic. 1). Before uke connects, escape with your left hand. With your right hand redirect uke's forearm (pic. 2-3). With your left hand take over uke's right wrist, pull it forward, and execute kotegaeshi (pic. 4-10).

Hanmi handachi waza · ryote dori - sumi otoshi

Offer both hands for uke to grab (pic. 1-2). As uke approaches and connects, absorb uke in by pulling your left hand onto your center line. With your right hand enter into uke's right elbow pit and execute sumi otoshi (pic. 3-5).

Hanmi handachi waza · ryote dori - juji garami

Offer both hands for uke to grab (pic. 1). As uke approaches and connects, use your left hand to take over uke's left wrist and your right hand to take over uke's right wrist (pic. 2-3). Wrap uke's right over left arm, push the arm lock forward, and finish juji garami (pic. 4-9).

Hanmi handachi waza · ryote dori - kokyu nage #1

Offer both hands for uke to grab (pic. 1). Before uke applies firm grip, absorb uke forward and up into kuzushi (pic. 2-4). Swiftly bring your arms downward in a crescent trajectory and execute kokyu nage (pic. 5-9).

Hanmi handachi waza · ryote dori - kokyu nage #2

Another form of kokyu nage from ryote dori grip is by absorbing uke forward and down (pic. 1-5) and then changing the direction up, pushing uke out (pic. 6-10).

Hanmi handachi waza · ryote dori - kokyu nage #3

Offer both hands for uke to grab (pic. 1-2). As uke approaches and connects, use your left hand to redirect uke behind your back (pic. 3-4). With your right arm pull uke forward and execute kokyu nage (pic. 5-8).

Hanmi handachi waza · ryote dori - kokyu nage #4

Offer both hands for uke to grab. As uke approaches and connects, use both hands to pull uke up and almost directly onto yourself (pic. 1-5). To avoid head-on collision, lean forward and to the side. Simultaneously bring your hands all the way behind your back and finish kokyu nage (pic. 6-9).

Hanmi handachi waza · ushiro ryote dori - kotegaeshi

Offer your left hand for uke to grab katate tori aihanmi. At the moment of connection, pull uke to the side and behind (pic. 1-3). Once uke is behind, offer your right hand, palm up, for uke to grab (pic. 4-5). As uke catches your wrist, begin meguri into nikyo position and bring uke to the front (pic. 6-8). Take over uke's right wrist and finish kotegaeshi (pic. 9-12).

Hanmi handachi waza · ushiro ryote dori - juji garami

Offer your left hand for uke to grab katate tori aihanmi. At the moment of connection, pull uke to the side and behind (pic. 1-2). Once uke is behind, offer your right hand for uke to grab (pic. 3-4). Bring your right hand down and take over uke's right wrist. With your left hand take over uke's left wrist (pic. 5). Wrap uke's right over the left arm and finish juji garami (pic. 6-10).

Hanmi handachi waza · ushiro ryote dori - kokyu nage

Offer your left hand for uke to grab katate tori aihanmi. At the moment of connection, pull uke to the side and behind (pic. 1-3). Once uke is behind, offer your right hand onto uke's center line (pic. 4). As uke catches on, use both arms to pull uke forward and execute kokyu nage (pic. 5-10).

Hanmi handachi waza · ushiro ryo kata dori - kokyu nage

Offer your left shoulder for uke to grab with left hand (pic. 1-2). At the moment of connection, pull uke to the side and behind by pressing your left arm onto uke's left arm and turning your torso sideways (pic. 3-4). As uke is about to catch your other shoulder, lean forward as you would into a bow, and execute kokyu nage (pic. 5-10).

Katate Tori Aihanmi

Tachi waza are standing techniques. They are the most popular segment of aikido repertoire.

Tachi waza · katate tori aihanmi - kotegaeshi

Offer your right hand, palm up, for uke to grab (pic. 1-2). As uke approaches and connects, step back. With your left hand apply atemi and take over uke's wrist. Pull uke forward into kuzushi and finish kotegaeshi (pic. 3-10).

Tachi waza · katate tori aihanmi - ikkyo omote

Offer your left hand, thumb down, for uke to grab. As uke approaches to catch your hand, move back and off the line (pic. 1-3). At the moment of connection, absorb uke further in and take over uke's wrist. With your right hand, take control of uke's elbow, enter forward, and finish ikkyo omote (pic. 4-9).

Tachi waza · katate tori aihanmi - ikkyo ura

Offer your left hand for uke to grab. As uke approaches to catch your hand, step back and raise your left hand. As uke connects, take over uke's wrist and elbow and begin to pivot (pic. 1-4). Continue to pivot, descend into seiza, and finish ikkyo ura (pic. 5-10).

Tachi waza · katate tori aihanmi - nikyo omote

Offer your left hand, thumb down, for uke to grab. As uke approaches, move back and off the line (pic. 1-3). As uke connects, use your right hand to take control of uke's elbow and enter forward (pic. 4). With your left hand, take over uke's left palm and set up nikyo hold (pic. 5-6). Finish nikyo omote in a circular motion downward (pic. 6-9). At the end finish nikyo omote pin (pic. 10).

Tachi waza · katate tori aihanmi - nikyo ura

Offer your right hand, thumb down, for uke to grab (pic. 1-2). As uke connects, simultaneously wrap your right hand around uke's wrist and place your left hand over uke's hold (pic. 3-4). Tighten your wrap around uke's wrist and execute nikyo ura (pic. 5-8).

Tachi waza · katate tori aihanmi - sankyo omote

Offer your left hand in a sankyo position for uke to grab (pic. 1-2). As uke approaches, take over uke's palm and simultaneously step back. With your right hand regrab uke's wrist (pic. 3-5). Move back while swiftly bringing the sankyo hold downward (pic. 6-9). Finish sankyo pin standing (pic. 10).

Tachi waza · katate tori aihanmi - sankyo ura

Offer your right hand in a sankyo position for uke to grab (pic. 1-2). As uke connects, take over uke's palm and regrab it with your left hand. With your right hand take over uke's elbow, descend into half position, and place uke's palm onto your left knee (pic. 3-6). Without removing uke's palm from your knee, move your left foot sideways and push uke back. Return to the front into seiza, bring uke with you, and finish sankyo ura pin (pic. 7-10).

Tachi waza · katate tori aihanmi - yonkyo

Offer your right hand for uke to grab (pic. 1-2). As uke approaches and connects, move back. Simultaneously take over uke's wrist, add left hand grip onto uke's forearm, and step forward (pic. 3-5). Apply yonkyo in a diagonal trajectory and finish yonkyo pin (pic. 6- 9).

Explore Aikido Vol. 1

Tachi waza · katate tori aihanmi - gokyo

Offer your left hand in a hyper extended sankyo position for uke to grab (pic. 1-2). As uke approaches and connects, unfold your left forearm with meguri, step back, and with your right hand take over uke's elbow (pic. 3-5). Execute gokyo (pic. 6-10). This gokyo resembles spiral vacuum tube or a funnel into which uke gets sucked in.

Tachi waza · katate tori aihanmi - shiho nage

Offer your left hand, palm up, for uke to grab (pic. 1). As uke approaches and connects, take over uke's wrist, move back, draw uke in, and add your right hand to the hold (pic. 2-3). Use the momentum to bring uke behind. Unfold uke's arm and finish shiho nage by bringing the hold down and projecting the throw forward (pic. 6-9).

Explore Aikido Vol. 1

Tachi waza · katate tori aihanmi - irimi nage

Offer your left hand, palm up, for uke to grab. As uke approaches, move back (pic. 1-3). Once uke is in a close distance zone, move forward. With your right forearm, enter onto uke's center line and execute irimi nage (pic. 4-8).

Tachi waza · katate tori aihanmi - yoko irimi

Offer your left hand for uke to grab. As uke approaches and connects, step back and off the line. Simultaneously bring your left arm in a circular motion in front of uke's face (pic. 1-4). With your right hand, continue to draw uke forward. At the same time unfold your left arm onto uke's center line and finish yoko irimi (pic. 5-8).

Explore Aikido Vol. 1

Tachi waza · katate tori aihanmi - sumi otoshi

Offer your left hand, thumb down, for uke to grab (pic. 1). As uke connects, use your left hand to take over uke's right wrist, apply yonkyo hold, and pivot (pic. 2-4). As uke comes around, keep holding yonkyo and with your right hand apply atemi (pic. 5). Slide your right hand into uke's right elbow pit and finish sumi otoshi (pic. 6-9).

Tachi waza · katate tori aihanmi - sumi otoshi #2

Offer your left hand, palm up, for uke to grab (pic. 1). As uke approaches and connects, with meguri, pull uke forward, up, and sideways (pic. 1-3). Once uke is in kuzushi, finish sumi otoshi (pic. 4-8).

Explore Aikido Vol. 1

Tachi waza · katate tori aihanmi - tai otoshi

Offer your left hand, thumb down, for uke to grab (pic. 1). As uke connects, use your left hand to take over uke's right wrist. Apply yonkyo hold and pivot (pic. 1-3). As uke follows, keep holding yonkyo and stretch uke's arm sideways. Enter under and into uke's right armpit and finish tai otoshi (pic. 4-9).

Tachi waza · katate tori aihanmi - ude kime nage omote

Offer your right hand, palm up, for uke to grab (pic. 1). As uke approaches and connects, take over uke's wrist, move back, and bring uke in and then sideways (pic. 2-4). With your left arm enter under and forward against uke's arm and finish ude kime nage omote (pic. 5-7).

Tachi waza · katate tori aihanmi - ude kime nage ura

Offer your right hand, palm up, for uke to grab (pic. 1). As uke approaches and connects, take over uke's wrist, step back, and pull uke forward (pic. 2-3). With your left arm enter under and against uke's arm and finish ude kime nage ura (pic. 4-8).

Tachi waza · katate tori aihanmi - ude kime osae

Offer your right hand, thumb down, for uke to grab (pic. 1). Step back and for a moment apply ikkyo hold on uke's arm (pic. 2-3). Wrap your left arm over uke's right arm (pic. 4). Execute ude kime osae by pressing onto uke's elbow and rotating your hips sideways (pic. 5-8).

Tachi waza · katate tori aihanmi - koshi nage

Offer your right hand for uke to grab (pic. 1). At the moment of connection, your hand should be in a sankyo position (pic. 2). Step back and pull uke up and onto yourself. At the same time, with left hand applying atemi, half squat and load uke onto your hips (pic. 3-6). Rise and execute koshi nage (pic. 7-9).

Tachi waza · katate tori aihanmi - kaiten nage

Offer your left hand, palm up, for uke to grab (pic. 1). As uke connects, use your left hand to take over uke's right wrist. Apply yonkyo hold and pivot (pic. 1-3). As uke follows and comes around, use your right hand to apply atemi and pass under uke's right arm (pic. 4-7). Step back, pull uke downward, and simultaneously take control of uke's neck (pic. 8-9). Bring uke's right arm up and finish kaiten nage (pic. 11-12).

Tachi waza · katate tori aihanmi - nikyo irimi

Offer your right hand, palm down, for uke to grab. As uke approaches and connects, move back. With meguri absorb uke in (pic. 1-5). With your right forearm close uke's center line and finish nikyo irimi (pic. 6-8).

Tachi waza · katate tori aihanmi - shiho nage irimi

Offer your right hand, palm up, for uke to grab (pic. 1). As uke approaches and connects, move back. Flex your palm up. From inside out, encircle uke's forearm and draw uke under your right arm (pic. 2-4). Bring uke behind and finish shiho nage irimi (pic. 5-8).

Tachi waza · katate tori aihanmi - kokyu nage

Offer your right hand, palm down, for uke to grab. Before uke is able to connect, begin to step back. Simultaneously lift your right hand (pic. 1-3). As uke is about to pass by, add your left hand onto uke's triceps, push forward, and execute kokyu nage (pic. 4-8).

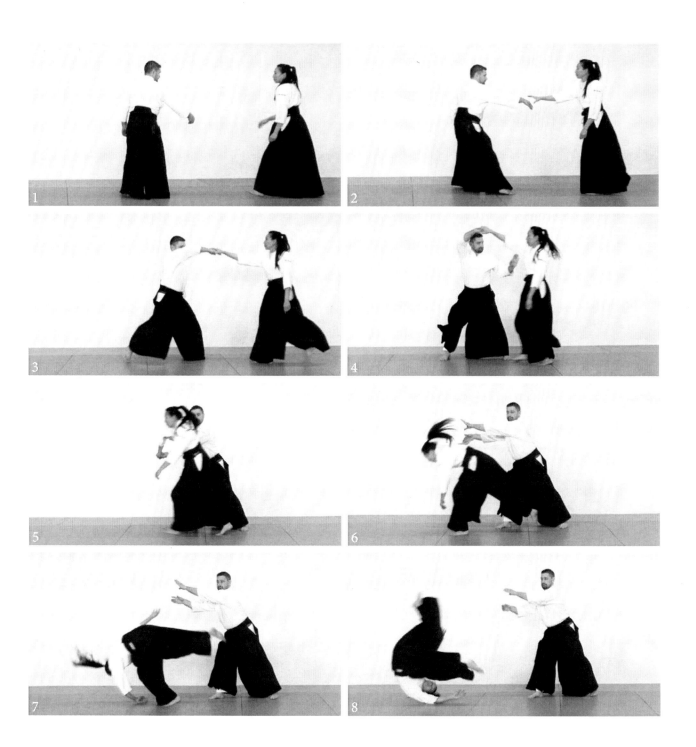

Katate Tori Gyakuhanmi

Tachi waza · katate tori gyakuhanmi - nikyo ura

Offer your left hand, thumb up, for uke to grab (pic. 1). As uke connects, open the hold sideways. Use your right hand to apply atemi and move uke off the line (pic, 2-3). With your left hand, take over uke's wrist. Execute nikyo ura and simultaneously descend into seiza (pic. 4-8). Apply vise lock and nikyo ura finish pin (pic. 9-12).

Tachi waza · katate tori gyakuhanmi - sankyo omote

Offer your left hand for uke to grab (pic. 1). As uke and connects, open the hold sideways. Use your right hand to apply atemi and move uke off the line (pic. 2-3). Take over uke's wrist and take control of sankyo hold (pic. 4-6). Finish sankyo by moving back and sideways (pic. 7-9). Finish sankyo pin standing (pic. 10).

Tachi waza · katate tori gyakuhanmi - yonkyo

Offer your left hand, palm up, for uke to grab. At the moment of connection, your palm should be almost in a kotegaeshi position; take over uke's wrist and open the hold sideways. With your right hand apply atemi (pic. 1-3). With both hands, take control of yonkyo hold and finish the technique in a diagonal trajectory (pic. 4-8). Finish yonkyo pin standing (pic. 9).

Tachi waza · katate tori gyakuhanmi - kotegaeshi

Offer your left hand, palm up, for uke to grab. At the moment of connection your hand should be in a thumb down position, with the thumb over uke's wrist (pic. 1-2). Take over uke's wrist, pull uke forward into kuzushi, and execute kotegaeshi (pic. 3-9).

Tachi waza · katate tori gyakuhanmi - shiho nage

Offer your left hand, thumb down, for uke to grab. As uke approaches and connects, move back. Take over uke's palm/wrist and pull it in toward your center (pic. 1-3). Add your right hand to the hold, lock uke's arm, and bring uke behind (pic. 4-6). Fold uke's arm and finish shiho nage (pic. 7-10).

Tachi waza · katate tori gyakuhanmi - irimi nage

Offer your left hand for uke to grab. As uke approaches and attempts to catch your hand, shift back and fold your left arm before uke is able to grab it (pic. 1-3). As uke is in full speed, step forward. With your right palm enter onto uke's center line and execute irimi nage (pic. 4-7).

Tachi waza · katate tori gyakuhanmi - yoko irimi

Offer your left hand, palm down, for uke to grab. As uke approaches and connects, move back and off the line. Bring your arm toward your center and absorb uke forward (pic. 1-4). Once uke passes by, unfold your arm onto uke's center line and finish yoko irimi (pic. 5-8).

Tachi waza · katate tori gyakuhanmi - tai otoshi

Offer your right hand for uke to grab (pic. 1). As uke approaches and connects, move back and bring your arm toward your center (pic. 1-3). Step forward and with your left arm enter under and into uke's left armpit, and finish tai otoshi (pic. 4-10).

Tachi waza · katate tori gyakuhanmi - koshi nage

Offer your right hand, thumb up, for uke to grab. As uke approaches and connects, step back, and pull your right hand toward your center. With your left hand apply atemi (pic. 1-2). Half squat, load uke onto your hips, rise and finish koshi nage (pic. 3-9).

Tachi waza · katate tori gyakuhanmi - kaiten nage

Offer your left hand for uke to grab. At the moment of connection open the hold sideways and use your right hand to apply atemi (pic. 1-3). With a circular motion of your left forearm, pull uke forward and down toward the mat. With your right hand, take control of uke's neck. Hold uke's neck down and arm up (pic. 4-7). Step in, push uke's arm forward, and finish kaiten nage (pic. 8-9).

Tachi waza · katate tori gyakuhanmi - kotegaeshi shiho nage

Offer your right hand, palm down, for uke to grab. At the moment of connection, your palm should be up (pic. 1-2). Lift your forearm to your eye level. This loosens and creates an opening in uke's grip. Slide your left hand into uke's grip and take over uke's palm. Remove your right hand from the grip and regrab uke's palm (pic. 3-5). Finish kotegaeshi shiho nage by swiftly bringing the grip downward in a circular motion (pic. 6-10).

Explore Aikido Vol. 1

Tachi waza · katate tori gyakuhanmi - kokyu nage #1

Offer your right hand for uke to grab (pic. 1). As uke approaches and connects, step back and apply atemi with your left hand (pic. 2-3). Continue to pull uke forward, step off the line, then turn around and position yourself under uke's arm (pic. 4-5). Project the throw forward and finish kokyu nage (pic. 6-8).

Tachi waza · katate tori gyakuhanmi - kokyu nage #2

Offer your left hand, palm down, for uke to grab (pic. 1). As uke approaches and connects, shift off the line and bring your left elbow and forearm forward and up (pic. 2-3). Once uke is in kuzushi, step forward and finish kokyu nage (pic. 4-9).

Katate Ryote Dori

Tachi waza · katate ryote dori - ikkyo omote

Offer your left hand for uke to grab (pic. 1). As uke approaches and connects, you should be pivoting (pic. 2-3). As uke follows and comes around, take over uke's left wrist and elbow. Simultaneously descend into seiza and finish ikkyo omote (pic. 4- 8).

Tachi waza · katate ryote dori - nikyo ura

Offer your right hand for uke to grab (pic. 1). As uke approaches to grab your arm, begin to pivot (pic. 2-4). As uke comes around, wrap your right hand around uke's right forearm. Place your left palm onto uke's right hand to prevent uke from letting go (pic. 5). Push the whole grip behind uke and execute nikyo ura (pic. 6-9).

Explore Aikido Vol. 1

Tachi waza · katate ryote dori - sankyo omote

Offer your left hand for uke to grab (pic. 1). As uke approaches and connects, step forward at 90° to uke's direction (pic. 2-3). Once uke is in kuzushi, with your right hand take over uke's left wrist. Slide your left arm under uke's left arm and through an elbow lock bring uke behind (pic. 4-5). Once uke comes around finish sankyo omote and apply sankyo pin standing (pic. 6- 9).

Tachi waza · katate ryote dori - gokyo

Offer your hand for uke to grab. As uke approaches and connects, start pivoting (pic. 1-4). As uke comes around, use your left hand to take over uke's left wrist. With your right hand take over uke's left elbow. Move back and execute gokyo (pic. 5-9).

Tachi waza · katate ryote dori - kotegaeshi

Offer your left hand for uke to grab (pic. 1). As uke approaches and connects, begin to pivot (pic. 1-3). When uke comes around, with your left forearm meguri change uke's direction. With your right hand take over uke's right wrist (pic. 4). Pull uke into kuzushi and execute kotegaeshi (pic. 5-9).

Tachi waza · katate ryote dori - shiho nage

Offer your left hand for uke to grab (pic. 1). As uke approaches and connects, use your left hand to take over uke's left wrist and pivot (pic. 1-4). As uke comes around add your right hand to the shiho nage hold, pass under uke's arm, and finish shiho nage (pic. 5-10).

Tachi waza · katate ryote dori - irimi nage

Offer your right hand, palm down, for uke to grab (pic. 1). As uke approaches, move back. At the moment of connection, your hand should end up in a palm up position and in between both of uke's forearms (pic. 2). Absorb uke forward by simultaneous meguri, and by bringing the hold in and up (pic. 3-4). Once uke is in kuzushi, close uke's center line, move in, and finish irimi nage (pic. 5-8).

Tachi waza · katate ryote dori - yoko irimi

This static form of yoko irimi is trained mainly for studying purposes. It forces trainees to analyze and apply all the necessary elements to make the technique work.

Offer your forearm in gokyo position. Uke applies strong two-hand grip (pic. 1). Turn your hips toward uke and bring your elbow toward your center. While keeping your elbow on your center line, turn your hips away. Simultaneously apply meguri. This causes uke to move forward (pic. 2-4). Close uke's center line with your elbow, unfold your arm, and finish yoko irimi (pic. 5-8).

Tachi waza · katate ryote dori - ude kime nage

Offer your left hand for uke to grab (pic. 1). As uke approaches and connects, begin to pivot (pic. 1-4). As uke comes around, redirect uke sideways, step forward, and execute ude kime nage (pic. 5-10).

Tachi waza · katate ryote dori - koshi nage

Offer your left hand, palm down, for uke to grab (pic. 1). As uke approaches and connects, bring your forearm up and step forward (pic. 2-4). Once uke is in kuzushi, load uke onto your hips (pic. 5). Rise, step back, and execute koshi nage (pic. 6-9).

Explore Aikido Vol. 1

Tachi waza · katate ryote dori - juji garami

Offer your left hand for uke to grab (pic. 1). As uke approaches and connects, begin to pivot (pic. 1-3). As uke comes around, separate his grip by taking control over both of uke's wrists (pic. 4-5). Wrap uke's right arm over uke's left arm, step forward, and execute juji garami (pic. 6-9).

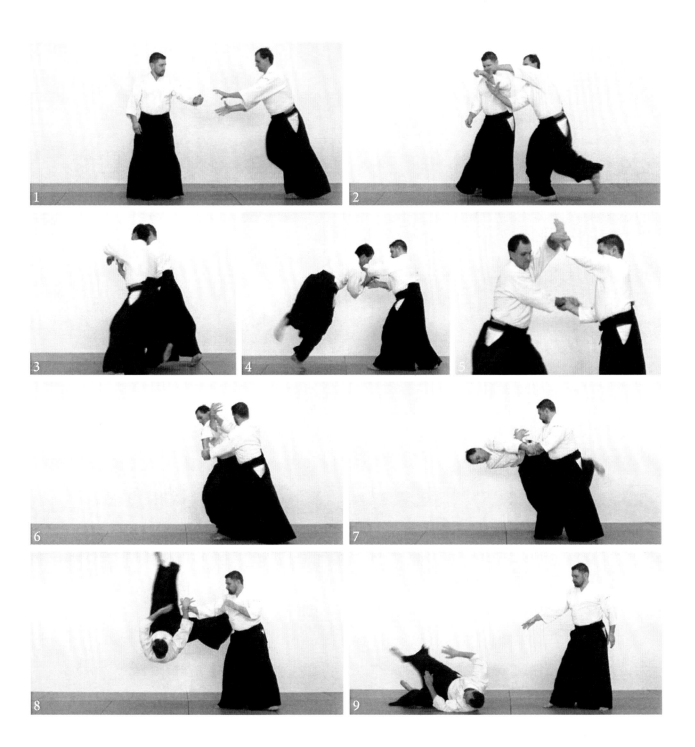

Tachi waza · katate ryote dori - nikyo irimi

Offer your left hand for uke to grab (pic. 1). As uke approaches and connects, begin to pivot (pic. 1-4). As uke comes around, move back. With meguri pull uke up and under your left arm (pic. 5-6). Once uke is next to you, close uke's center line and finish nikyo irimi (pic. 7-10).

Tachi waza · katate ryote dori - shiho nage sankyo irimi

Offer your left hand in a sankyo position for uke to grab (pic. 1). As uke approaches move back and off the line. At the moment of connection your hand should be in a sankyo position and up high (pic. 2-3). Pass above and behind uke's head to set up shiho nage sankyo. With your right hand close uke's center line and step forward (pic. 4-9).

Tachi waza · katate ryote dori - kotegaeshi shiho nage

Offer your right hand, palm down, for uke to grab. At the moment of connection, your palm should be at your eye level (pic. 1-3). Use your left hand to take over uke's left palm. Remove your right hand from the grip, regrab uke's palm from the top, and finish kotegaeshi shiho nage (pic. 4-9).

Tachi waza · katate ryote dori - ude kime koshi nage

Offer your right hand, thumb up, for uke to grab (pic. 1). As uke connects, move back and off the line and with meguri redirect uke sideways (pic. 2-3). Enter with your left arm under uke's arms, half squat, and load uke onto your hips (pic. 4-5). Rise, step back, and execute koshi nage (pic. 6-9).

Explore Aikido Vol. 1

Tachi waza · katate ryote dori - kokyu nage #1

Offer your left hand in a nikyo position for uke to grab (pic. 1). As uke approaches and connects, begin to fold your arm into a shiho nage position while stepping forward (pic. 2-4). Step through, unfold your forearm into nikyo position, and execute kokyu nage (pic. 5-8).

Tachi waza · katate ryote dori - kokyu nage #2

Offer your left arm in a nikyo position for uke to grab (pic. 1). As uke approaches and connects, step back. Use your right hand to pull uke up and forward (pic. 2-4). Add your left hand onto uke's right arm triceps, push forward, and finish kokyu nage (pic. 5-8).

Tachi waza · katate ryote dori - kokyu nage #3

Offer your left hand, palm up, for uke to grab (pic. 1-2). As uke approaches and connects, begin meguri with your left forearm and pull uke up (pic. 3-5). Step forward and finish kokyu nage (pic. 6-8).

Ryote Dori

Tachi waza · ryote dori - ikkyo omote

Offer both hands for uke to grab (pic. 1). As uke approaches and connects, simultaneously step back. Use your right hand to scoop uke's right forearm and your left hand to take over uke's right elbow (pic. 1-3). Step forward and execute ikkyo omote (pic. 4-9).

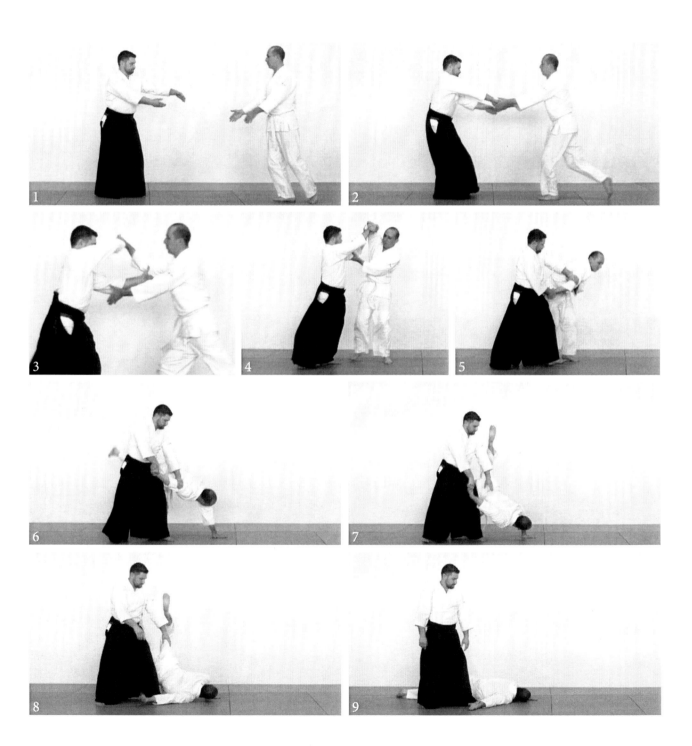

Tachi waza · ryote dori - nikyo ura

Offer both hands for uke to grab. As uke approaches and connects, shift sideways. Open uke's left arm and use your right hand to apply atemi (pic. 1-3). Take over uke's right forearm and set up nikyo ura (pic. 4-5). Use your left hand to apply atemi into uke's ribs and chin. Return your hand to the nikyo hold (pic. 6-8). Execute nikyo ura by turning your hips and upper body sideways and downward (pic. 9-10). Once uke takes ukemi, release uke's arm and finish the nikyo ura standing (pic. 12).

Tachi waza · ryote dori - sankyo omote

Offer both hands for uke to grab. As uke approaches and connects, use your right hand to open uke's left arm sideways and with your left hand apply atemi (pic. 1-2). Take control of uke's left forearm and set up a sankyo hold (pic. 3-5). Move back and finish sankyo omote (pic. 6-7). Finish sankyo pin standing (pic. 8).

Tachi waza · ryote dori - kotegaeshi

Offer both hands for uke to grab. As uke approaches and is about to connect, move back and off the line. Use your right hand to redirect uke's right hand grip (pic. 1-4). With your left hand take over uke's right wrist and pull it forward. Once uke is in kuzushi, change the direction and execute kotegaeshi (pic. 5-8).

Explore Aikido Vol. 1

Tachi waza · ryote dori - shiho nage

Offer both arms for uke to grab. As uke approaches and connects, move sideways and pull your left hand toward your center. Use your right hand to apply atemi, then take control of uke's right elbow (pic. 1-4). Lock uke's elbow and by the counter movement of your hands pull uke behind your back (pic. 5-6). As uke comes around, slide both hands and take over uke's right wrist (pic. 7). Step in and finish shiho nage (pic. 8-10).

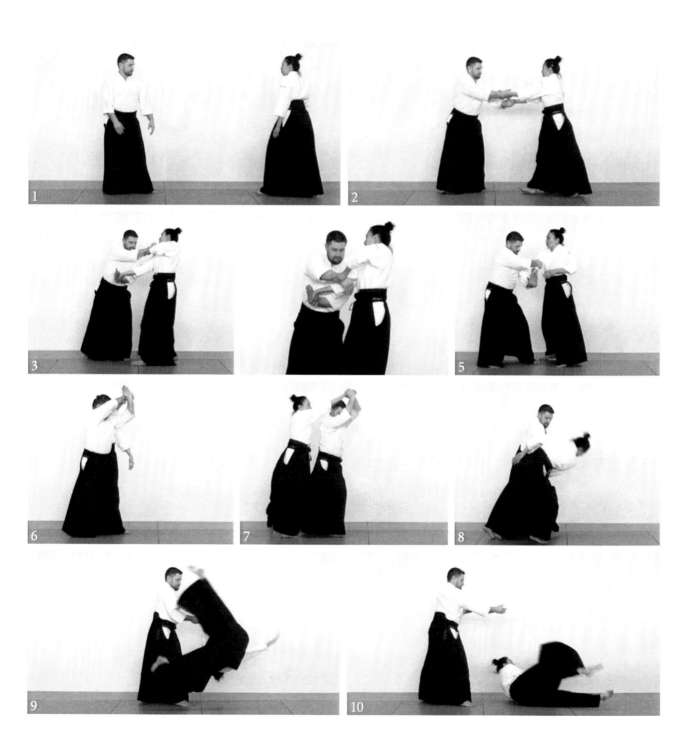

Tachi waza · ryote dori - irimi nage

Offer both arms for uke to grab. As uke approaches and is about to connect, move back and off the line. Use your right hand to take over uke's right wrist. Place your left hand onto uke's back (pic. 1-4). Bring uke forward. Use uke's right palm to close uke's center line and finish irimi nage (pic. 5-7).

Explore Aikido Vol. 1

Tachi waza · ryote dori - yoko irimi

Offer both arms for uke to grab. As uke approaches and connects, step back. Draw uke in by stretching uke's left arm forward and down. Use your right elbow to enter onto uke's center line and finish yoko irimi (pic. 1-9).

Tachi waza · ryote dori - sumi otoshi

Offer both hands for uke to grab. As uke approaches, change your profile and let uke catch your right hand. With your left hand apply atemi (pic. 1-2). Slide your left hand into uke's elbow pit. Push uke's elbow up, so that uke is in kuzushi, step forward, and finish sumi otoshi (pic. 3-8).

Tachi waza · ryote dori - tai otoshi

Offer both hands for uke to grab. As uke approaches, change your profile and let uke catch your right hand (pic. 1-2). Stretch uke's left arm. Use your left arm to enter under and into uke's armpit and finish tai otoshi (pic. 3-9).

Tachi waza · ryote dori - ude kime nage

Offer both hands for uke to grab. As uke approaches and connects, pull your left hand toward your center and use your right hand to take over uke's right wrist (pic, 1-3). Release your left hand from uke's grip, enter under and against uke's right arm, and finish ude kime nage (pic. 4-10).

Tachi waza · ryote dori - koshi nage

Offer both hands for uke to grab. As uke approaches and connects, shift back. Use your left hand to redirect uke toward your back and your right hand to pull uke up and forward (pic. 1-3). Half squat and load uke onto your hips (pic. 4-5). Rise, move out, and finish koshi nage (pic. 6-8).

Tachi waza · ryote dori - tenchi nage #1

Offer both hands for uke to grab. As uke approaches and connects, absorb uke in by moving back. Pull your left hand toward your center and use your right hand to stretch uke up (pic. 1-4). Bring your left hand down and sideways. Use your right hand close uke's center line and execute tenchi nage (pic. 5-7).

Explore Aikido Vol. 1

Tachi waza · ryote dori - tenchi nage #2

Offer both hands for uke to grab. As uke approaches and connects, shift back and absorb uke onto yourself. Use your left forearm to pull uke up and your right hand to redirect uke sideways and down (pic. 1-4). Execute tenchi nage by bringing uke down with your right hand and pushing uke out with your left (pic. 5-8).

Tachi waza · ryote dori - juji garami

Offer both hands for uke to grab (pic. 1). As uke approaches and is about to connect, move back and off the line. With your right hand scoop uke's right forearm and with your left hand take over uke's left forearm (pic. 1-3). Wrap uke's arms one over the other, step in, and execute juji garami (pic. 4-9).

Tachi waza · ryote dori - kokyu nage #1

Offer both hands for uke to grab (pic. 1-2). As uke approaches and connects, step back and off the line. With your elbows leading, pull uke forward and up (pic. 3-4). Once uke is passing by and in kuzushi, bring your forearms down and forward in a circular motion, and finish kokyu nage (pic. 5-8).

Tachi waza · ryote dori - kokyu nage #2

Offer both hands for uke to grab (pic. 1-2). As uke approaches and connects, move back and off the line and pull uke up (pic. 3-5). As uke passes by, continue to raise your arms until uke loses connection with the ground below his feet. Then lower your arms (pic. 6-10).

Tachi waza · ryote dori - kokyu nage #3

Offer both hands for uke to grab (pic. 1-2). As uke approaches and connects, shift back and sideways. Use your left hand to redirect and pull uke behind (pic. 1-4). As uke comes around, simultaneously step forward, unfold your right hand, and send uke forward into kokyu nage (pic. 5-7).

Mune Dori

Tachi waza · mune dori - ikkyo omote

Begin in right profile stance. As uke approaches and tries to grab your chest, step back and off the line. Use your right hand to deflect uke's left forearm and your left hand to apply atemi (pic. 1-4). Use your left hand to scoop and take over uke's left wrist. Place your right hand onto uke's left elbow, step forward, and finish ikkyo omote in seiza (pic. 5-9).

Tachi waza · mune dori - nikyo ura

Begin in right profile stance. As uke approaches and grabs your chest, step back off the line. With your left hand apply atemi and from the top take over uke's left hand (pic. 1-3). Step back again while holding uke's left hand grip. With right hand apply atemi into uke's ribs and chin (pic. 4-6). Fold and add your right hand to nikyo ura hold and begin descending into seiza. Apply nikyo vise and nikyo ura pin at the end (pic. 5-12).

Explore Aikido Vol. 1

Tachi waza · mune dori - sankyo omote

Begin in right profile stance. As uke approaches and grabs your chest, step back off the line. Use your left hand to apply atemi and from the top, take over uke's left hand (pic. 1-4). Step back again and pull uke's grip off your gi. With your right hand take over uke's left wrist, execute sankyo omote, and finish sankyo pin standing (pic. 5- 10).

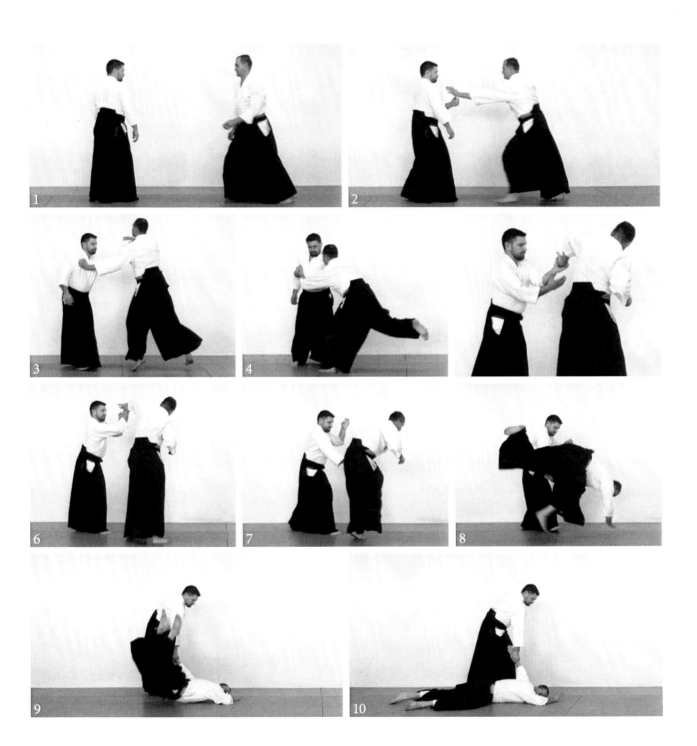

Tachi waza · mune dori - shiho nage

Begin in left profile stance. As uke approaches and tries to grab your chest, step back. Use your left hand to deflect uke's left forearm and take over uke's right wrist. Use your right hand to apply atemi (pic. 1-3). Add your right hand to uke's right wrist. Step back and pull uke forward toward your center. Start turning under uke's arm and descend into half position (pic. 4-6). Unfold uke's arm and finish shiho nage (pic. 7-9).

Tachi waza · mune dori - kotegaeshi

Begin in right profile stance. As uke approaches and tries to grab your chest, step back. Use your left hand to apply atemi and immediately deflect uke's arm from outside in (pic. 1-4). Step back again, with your right hand take over uke's left wrist, and execute kotegaeshi (pic. 5-10).

Tachi waza · mune dori - nanakyo

Begin in left profile stance. As uke approaches and tries to grab your chest, move back and off the line. From below take over uke's right wrist (pic. 1-3). Add your right hand to the hold (pic. 4). Press uke's hand and forearm together and begin to descent into seiza (pic. 5-7). Finish nanakyo pin by squeezing uke's hand and forearm together. Additionally pull uke's wrist up and push uke's forearm down (pic. 8).

Tachi waza · mune dori - irimi nage

Begin in left profile stance. As uke approaches and tries to grab your chest, step back. With your right hand apply atemi and immediately deflect uke's right forearm from outside in (pic. 1-4). As uke gets closer, step forward, and finish irimi nage (pic. 5-8).

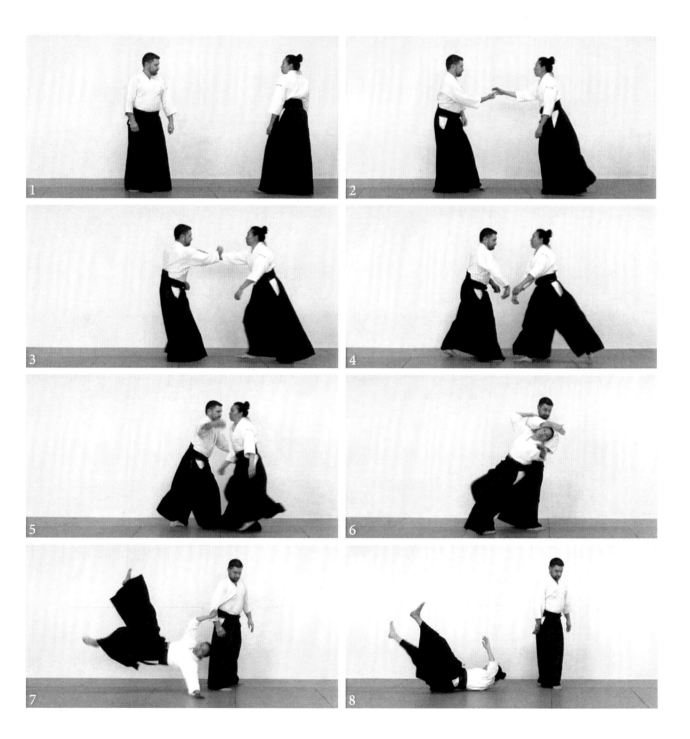

Tachi waza · mune dori - yoko irimi

Begin in left profile stance. As uke approaches and tries to grab your chest, move back and off the line. With your right hand take over uke's forearm from outside in (pic. 1-4). Pull uke forward. With your left elbow close uke's center line and finish yoko irimi (pic. 5-8).

Tachi waza · mune dori - ude kime nage

Begin in left profile stance. As uke approaches and tries to grab your chest, step back off the line. Use your right hand to take over uke's hand from outside (pic. 1-3). Stretch uke's arm and use your left hand to take control of uke's right elbow (pic. 4). Step forward and execute ude kime nage (pic. 5-8).

Tachi waza · mune dori - ude kime osae

Begin in left profile stance. As uke approaches and tries to grab your chest, move back and off the line. Use your right hand to take over uke's hand from outside (pic. 1-3). Stretch uke's arm and use your left hand to take control of uke's right elbow (pic. 4). Press uke's elbow down, execute ude kime osae, and finish ude kime osae pin (pic. 5- 8).

Tachi waza · mune dori - kaiten nage

Begin in left profile stance. As uke approaches and tries to grab your chest, move back and off the line. Use both hands to deflect uke's attack (pic. 1-3). Use your left hand to take control of uke's forearm, and your right hand to apply atemi and take hold of uke's neck (pic. 4-5). Simultaneously pull uke's neck down, step in, and push uke's arm forward (pic. 6-8).

Tachi waza · mune dori - ude garami

Begin in left profile stance. As uke approaches and tries to grab your chest, move back. From the bottom up take over uke's right elbow. Push it up and with your right hand apply atemi (pic. 1-4). In an elliptical trajectory flip uke's elbow forward and down. Pull uke to the mat and finish ude garami pin (pic. 5-8).

Tachi waza · mune dori - shiho nage sankyo

Begin in right profile stance. As uke approaches and tries to grab your chest, move back and off the line. From the top, with your right hand, take over uke's left elbow. Push it down and forward while pivoting (pic. 1-5). Use both hands to take control of uke's elbow. Press it against your chest, shift sideways, and finish shiho nage sankyo (pic. 6-8).

Ryo Mune Dori

Tachi waza · ryo mune dori - ikkyo omote

Begin in left profile stance. As uke approaches and tries to grab your lapels, step back and use your right hand to apply atemi (pic. 1-3). Slide your right hand in between uke's arms and cut off uke's right hand grip (pic. 4-6). Take over uke's wrist and elbow, and finish ikkyo omote standing (pic. 7-10).

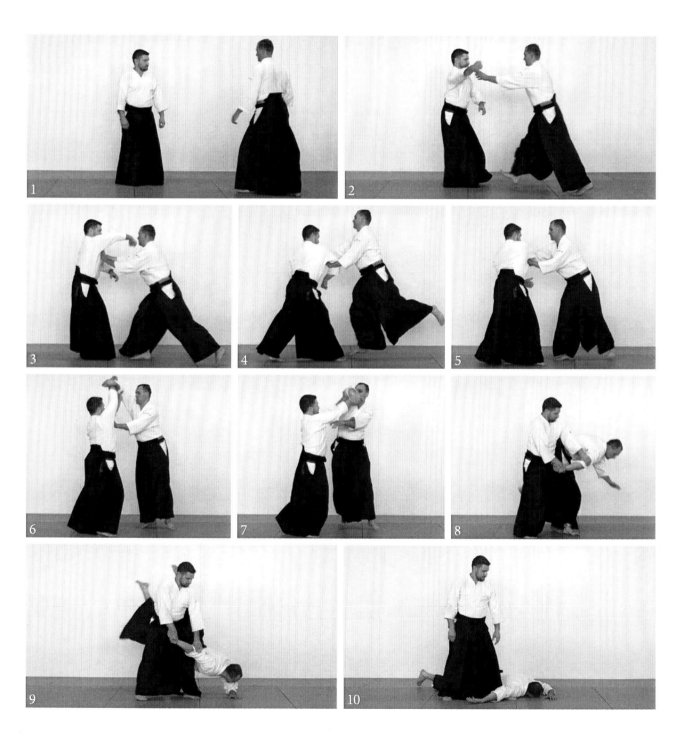

Tachi waza · ryo mune dori - nikyo omote

Begin in right profile stance. As uke approaches and tries to grab your lapels, step back. Use your left hand to apply atemi and immediately take over uke's left hand (pic. 1-3). Pull uke's left hand grip off and keep it in nikyo hold. Use your right hand to take control of uke's left elbow, step in, and finish nikyo omote in seiza (pic. 4-8).

Tachi waza · ryo mune dori - irimi nage

Begin in left profile stance. As uke approaches and tries to grab your lapels, shift slightly back to absorb and accelerate uke's attack (pic. 1-2). As uke gets close, step forward, use your right palm to close uke's center line, and finish irimi nage (pic. 3-8).

Tachi waza · ryo mune dori - ude kime irimi

Begin in left profile stance. As uke approaches and tries to grab your lapels, shift slightly back. As uke connects, immediately take control of both of uke's elbows (pic. 1-3). Absorb, extend and lock uke's arms. Step forward and push uke's arms up (pic. 4-5). Once uke is off the ground, release uke's elbows (pic. 6-8).

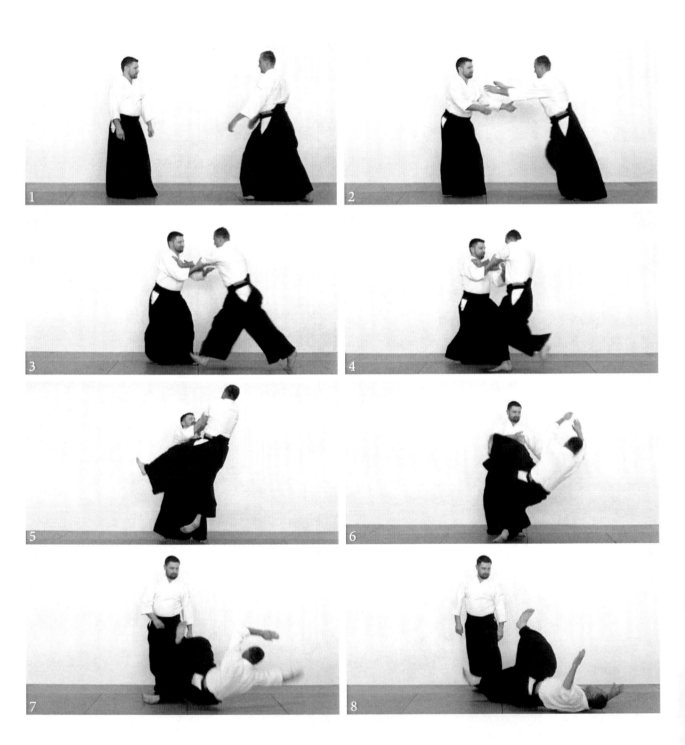

Tachi waza · ryo mune dori - kokyu nage #1

Begin in right profile stance. As uke approaches and tries to grab your lapels, execute mae geri, and take over uke's arms (pic. 1-3). Use your right hand to take control and pull down uke's left elbow. Use your left hand to push uke's right elbow up and sideways, and finish kokyu nage (pic. 4-8).

Tachi waza · ryo mune dori - kokyu nage #2

Begin in right profile stance. As uke approaches and tries to grab your lapels, use your right hand to apply atemi from the bottom up and in between uke's arms (pic. 1-3). Step back and wrap your right arm around uke's left elbow. Use your left hand to push uke's right elbow up and forward (pic. 4-8).

Tachi waza · ryo mune dori - kokyu nage #3

This kokyu nage is similar to the previous one. The difference is that the atemi is now coming in above uke's arms instead from the bottom.

Begin in right profile stance. As uke approaches and tries to grab your lapels, use your right hand to apply atemi from above uke's arms (pic. 1-2). Step back and use your right forearm to push uke's left elbow down. Use your left hand to push uke's right elbow up and forward (pic. 3-7).

Kata Tori Men Uchi

Tachi waza · kata tori men uchi - ikkyo omote

Begin in left profile stance. As uke approaches and attacks, shift slightly back and off the line. Use your left forearm to connect with uke's left forearm. Absorb uke's attack and use your right hand to take control of uke's left elbow (pic. 1-4). Simultaneously step forward, descend into seiza, and execute ikkyo omote (pic. 5-8).

Tachi waza · kata tori men uchi - nikyo omote

Begin in left profile stance. As uke approaches and attacks, use your left forearm to connect with uke's left elbow. Simultaneously step back and with meguri bring uke's left arm down (pic. 1-4). Use your right hand to take hold of uke's right palm and apply nikyo hold. Use your left hand to take control of uke's elbow, step forward, and finish nikyo omote in seiza (pic. 5-8).

Tachi waza · kata tori men uchi - sankyo omote

Begin in left profile stance. As uke approaches and attacks, shift back off the line. Use your left forearm to connect with uke's left elbow and your right hand to apply atemi. Take control of uke's striking arm and lock it against your body (pic, 1-3). Through an arm lock move uke behind. As uke comes around, finish sankyo omote (pic. 4-8).

Tachi waza · kata tori men uchi - irimi nage #1

Begin in right profile stance. As uke approaches and attempts to grab your shoulder and strike, turn away. Immediately start to pivot on your front foot and pull uke into motion (pic. 1-4). As uke comes around, with your left hand close uke's center line, step forward, and execute irimi nage (pic. 5-8).

Explore Aikido Vol. 1

Tachi waza · kata tori men uchi - irimi nage #2

Begin in right profile stance. As uke approaches and attacks, use your right forearm to connect with uke's right elbow. Simultaneously step back and with meguri bring uke's right arm down (pic. 1-3). Once uke is pulled into motion, close uke's center line over uke's left elbow. Step forward and finish irimi nage (pic. 5-8).

Tachi waza · kata tori men uchi - yoko irimi

Begin in left profile stance. As uke approaches and attacks, shift back off the line. Use your left forearm to connect with uke's left elbow. Fold your arm and absorb uke's attack (pic. 1-3). As uke gets close, unfold your left arm onto uke's center line, and execute yoko irimi (pic. 5-8).

Tachi waza · kata tori men uchi - sumi otoshi

Begin in right profile stance. As uke approaches and attacks, shift back off the line. With your right forearm connect with uke's right elbow and apply atemi with your left hand (pic. 1-2). Through an arm lock, move uke behind (pic. 3-5). As uke comes around, bring uke to the front through sankyo control. Unfold uke's arm from inside out and regrab uke's wrist. Use your right hand to apply atemi, enter into uke's elbow pit, and execute sumi otoshi (pic. 6-10).

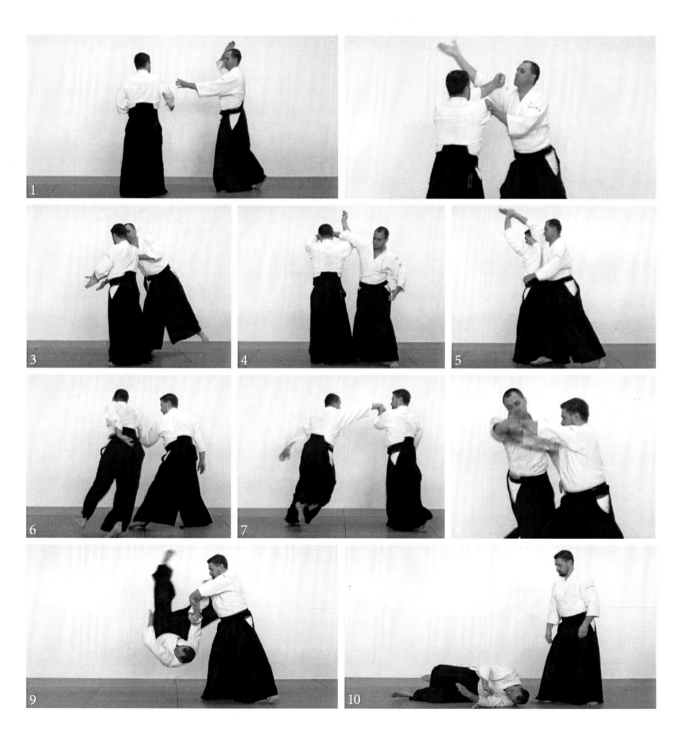

Tachi waza · kata tori men uchi - koshi nage.

Begin in left profile stance. As uke approaches and attacks, shift back off the line. Use your left forearm to connect with uke's left elbow and your right hand to apply atemi. Take over uke's striking arm. Lock it against your body and through an arm lock move uke behind (pic. 1-3). Half squat, load uke onto your hips, and executes koshi nage (pic. 5-8).

Explore Aikido Vol. 1

Tachi waza · kata tori men uchi - kaiten nage

Begin in right profile stance. As uke approaches and attacks, shift back off the line. Use your right forearm to connect with uke's right elbow and your left hand to apply atemi (pic. 1-3). Through an arm lock move uke behind (pic. 3-6). As uke comes around, through sankyo control bring uke down and toward your center. Use your right hand to take control of uke's neck (pic. 7-8). Step in and push uke's arm forward (pic. 9-10).

Tachi waza · kata tori men uchi - juji garami

Begin in right profile stance. As uke approaches and attacks, use your right forearm to connect with uke's right elbow. Simultaneously step back and with meguri pull uke's right arm down and. Use your left hand to cut off uke's left hand grip from the bottom and take over uke's both wrists (pic. 1-5). Wrap uke's right arm over uke's left arm, enter forward, and finish juji garami (pic. 6-8).

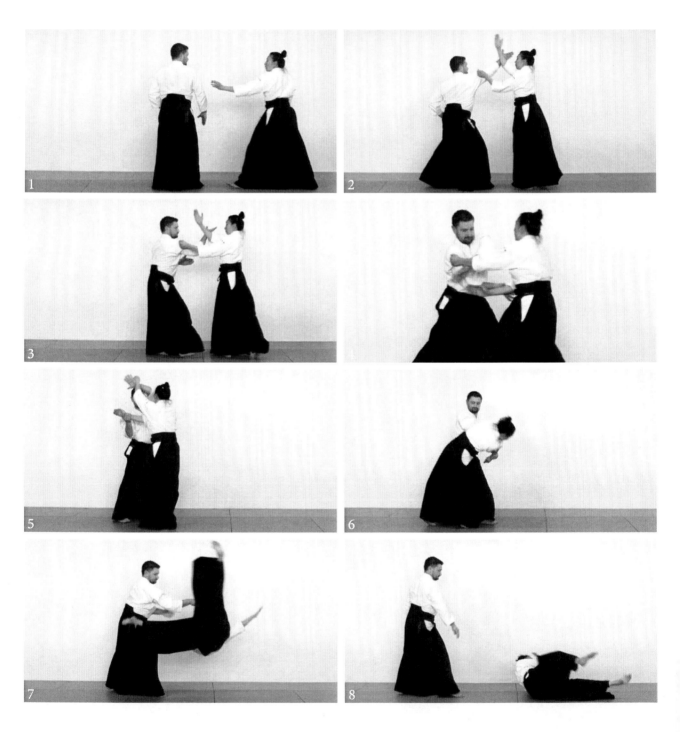

Explore Aikido Vol. 1

Tachi waza · kata tori men uchi - kotegaeshi shiho nage

Begin in left profile stance. As uke approaches and attacks, use your left forearm to connect with uke's left elbow. Redirect uke's strike and wrap your arm around both of uke's arms (pic. 1-5). Pull uke forward, change the direction, and execute kotegaeshi shiho nage (pic. 7-10).

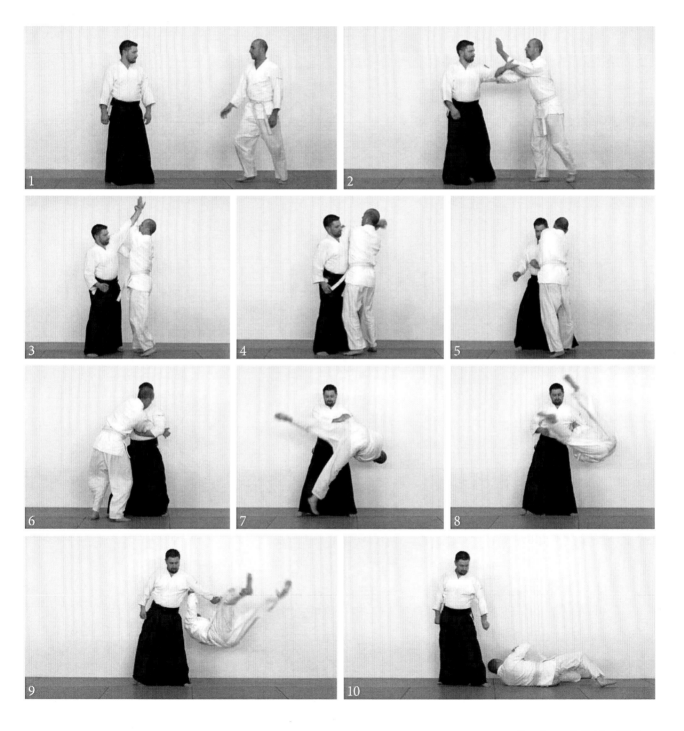

Tachi waza · kata tori men uchi - kokyu nage #1.

Begin in right profile stance. As uke approaches and attempts to grab your shoulder and strike, turn away, immediately pivot and pull uke into the motion (pic. 1-4). As uke comes around, with your left hand apply atemi (pic. 5). Step forward under uke's arm, descend into half position and finish kokyu nage (pic. 6-10).

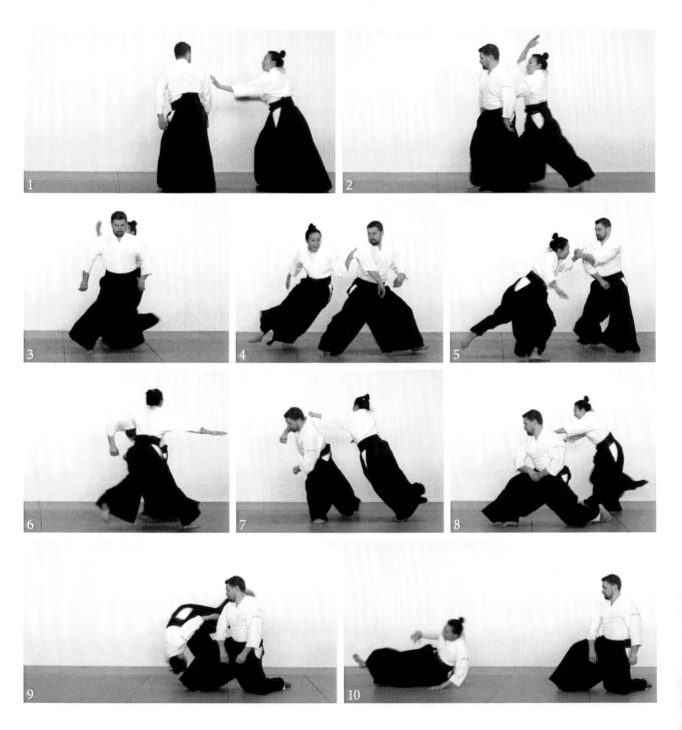

Explore Aikido Vol. 1

Tachi waza · kata tori men uchi - kokyu nage #2

Begin in left profile stance. As uke approaches and attacks, shift off the line. Use your left forearm to immediately connect with uke's striking arm (pic. 1-2). Step froward, descend into half position, and lead uke forward into kokyu nage (pic. 3-6).

Shomen Uchi

Tachi waza · shomen uchi - ikkyo omote

Begin in left profile stance. As uke approaches and attacks, move back and off the line. Use your left forearm to connect with uke's left forearm. Absorb uke's attack and take control of uke's left elbow with your right hand (pic. 1-4). Step forward and finish ikkyo omote in seiza (pic. 5-7).

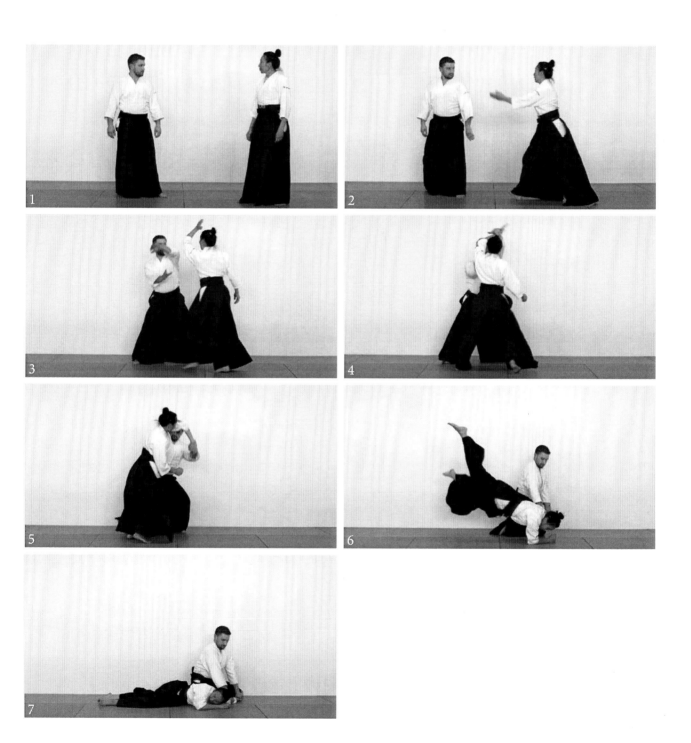

Tachi waza · shomen uchi - nikyo ura

Begin in right profile stance. As uke approaches and attacks, use your right hand to connect with uke's right forearm. With your left hand, take over uke's wrist from the bottom. Simultaneously step back and set up nikyo ura hold (pic. 1-5). Use your left hand to apply atemi and execute nikyo ura (pic. 6-9). Apply nikyo vise and nikyo ura pin (pic. 10-12).

Tachi waza · shomen uchi - sankyo omote

Begin in right profile stance. As uke approaches and attacks, use your right hand to connect with uke's right forearm. With your left hand take over uke's wrist from the bottom. Simultaneously step back and take control of sankyo hold with your left hand (pic. 1-5). Move back and execute sankyo omote (pic. 6-8).

Tachi waza · shomen uchi - kotegaeshi

Begin in right profile stance. As uke approaches and attacks, use your right hand to connect with uke's right forearm. With your left hand take over uke's wrist from the top. Simultaneously step back and draw uke forward into kuzushi (pic. 1-4). Change direction and execute kotegaeshi (pic. 5-8).

Tachi waza · shomen uchi - irimi nage #1

Begin in right profile stance. As uke approaches and attacks, use your right hand to connect with uke's right elbow. With meguri bring uke's arm down and sideways (pic. 1-4). Use your forearm to close uke's center line and finish irimi nage omote (pic. 5-8).

Tachi waza · shomen uchi - irimi nage #2

Begin in right profile stance. As uke approaches and attacks, use your right hand to apply atemi. Step forward off the line next to uke and take control of uke's elbow and neck (pic. 1-3). Pivot, close uke's center line with your right forearm, and finish irimi nage ura (pic. 4-8).

Explore Aikido Vol. 1

Tachi waza · shomen uchi - irimi nage #3

Begin in right profile stance. As uke approaches and attacks, use your right hand to block uke's elbow from the bottom. With your left hand enter directly onto uke's center line (pic. 1-3). Immediately move off the line, enter onto uke's center line, and finish irimi nage omote (pic. 4-7).

Tachi waza · shomen uchi - irimi nage #4

Begin in right profile stance. As uke approaches and attacks, apply atemi onto uke's center line and quickly pull out your hand. Simultaneously step back and off the line (pic. 1-4). As uke finishes shomen uchi, with your right forearm close uke's center line, and execute irimi nage omote (pic. 5-8).

Explore Aikido Vol. 1

Tachi waza · shomen uchi - yoko irimi

Begin in right profile stance. As uke approaches and attacks, use your right hand to connect with uke's forearm. Step back and enter onto uke's center line with your left elbow (pic. 1-4). As uke passes by, unfold your left arm and execute yoko irimi (pic. 5-8).

Tachi waza · shomen uchi - sumi otoshi

Begin in right profile stance. As uke approaches and attacks, step forward and use your left hand to apply atemi (pic. 1-3). Pivot, wrap your left arm over uke's arm, and lock uke's elbow (pic. 4). As uke comes around, use your right hand to apply atemi. Slide your hand into uke's elbow pit and finish sumi otoshi (pic. 5-9).

Tachi waza · shomen uchi - sudori nage

Begin in right profile stance. As uke approaches and attacks, shift back slightly (pic. 1-2). Move forward and descend under and into uke's legs (pic. 3-6). Continue to move forward and finish sudori nage in seiza (pic. 7-8).

Tachi waza · shomen uchi - ude kime nage ura

Begin in right profile stance. As uke approaches and attacks, step forward. Use your left hand to apply atemi and your right hand to connect with uke's elbow from the outside. Pivot (pic. 1-4). Lock uke's arm at the elbow, bring uke around, and finish ude kime nage ura (pic. 5-8).

Tachi waza · shomen uchi - koshi nage

Begin in right profile stance. As uke approaches and attacks, step forward and use your left hand to apply atemi (pic. 1-3). Pivot, wrap your left arm over uke's arm, and lock uke's elbow (pic. 4). As uke comes around, use your right hand to apply atemi. Move back and regrab uke's right wrist with your left hand. Half squat and load uke onto your hips (pic. 5-8). Rise, step back, and finish koshi nage (pic. 9-10).

Tachi waza · shomen uchi - kaiten nage

Begin in right profile stance. As uke approaches and attacks, step back. With your right forearm connect with uke's right elbow, then add your left forearm to uke's right elbow (pic. 1-4). Use your right hand to take control of uke's neck and your left forearm to control uke's right elbow (pic. 5). Pull uke's neck down, push uke's arm forward, and execute kaiten nage (pic. 6-8).

Yokomen Uchi

Tachi waza · yokomen uchi - ikkyo omote

Begin in left profile stance. As uke approaches and attacks, use your left hand to apply atemi. Step back, retract your left forearm, and control uke's right arm. With your right hand apply second atemi (pic. 1-5). With your right hand take over uke's right wrist. With your left hand take over uke's elbow. Step forward and finish ikkyo omote in seiza (pic. 6-10).

Tachi waza · yokomen uchi - nanakyo

Begin in left profile stance. As uke approaches and attacks, use your left hand to apply atemi onto uke's center line. Move sideways and open uke's right arm with your left forearm. With your right hand, apply second atemi (pic. 1-4). Use your right hand to take over uke's palm and your left hand to take over uke's wrist (pic. 5-6). Press together uke's palm and forearm, begin to descent into seiza, and finish nanakyo pin (pic. 7- 10).

Explore Aikido Vol. 1

Tachi waza · yokomen uchi - sankyo omote

Begin in left profile stance. As uke approaches and attacks, use your left hand to apply atemi. Step back, retract your left forearm, and control uke's right arm. With your right hand apply second atemi (pic. 1-4). With your right hand take over uke's right palm. Step back, use your left hand to regrab sankyo hold, and finish sankyo omote (pic. 5-9).

Tachi waza · yokomen uchi - yonkyo

Begin in left profile stance. As uke approaches and attacks, use your left hand to apply atemi. Step back, retract your left forearm, and control uke's right arm. With your right hand apply second atemi (pic. 1-4). With your right hand, take over uke's left wrist, add your left hand grip to uke's forearm, and finish yonkyo in seiza (pic. 5-9).

Tachi waza · yokomen uchi - gokyo #1

Begin in left profile stance. As uke approaches and attacks, use your left hand to apply atemi. Step back, retract your left forearm, and control uke's right arm. With your right hand apply second atemi (pic. 1-3). With your right hand take over uke's right wrist and step back. With your left hand take control of uke's right elbow and execute gokyo (pic. 4-8).

Tachi waza · yokomen uchi - gokyo #2

Begin in left profile stance. As uke approaches and attacks, use your left hand to apply atemi onto uke's center line. Simultaneously move sideways, use your left forearm to open uke's right arm, and your right hand to apply second atemi (pic. 1-3). Use your right hand to take over uke's wrist and your left hand to take over uke's elbow, descend into seiza, and finish standard gokyo (pic. 4-8).

Tachi waza · yokomen uchi - kotegaeshi

Begin in left profile stance. As uke approaches and attacks, step back and use your right hand to apply atemi (pic. 1-3). Deflect uke's yokomen uchi attack while stepping back (pic. 4-5). Take over uke's wrist with your left hand, bring uke forward into kuzushi, and execute kotegaeshi (pic. 6-10).

Tachi waza · yokomen uchi - shiho nage

Begin in left profile stance. As uke approaches and attacks, use your left hand to apply atemi. Step back and take control of uke's right wrist. With your right hand apply second atemi and add your right hand to uke's forearm (pic. 1-4). Pull uke forward, turn under uke's arm into half seated position, and finish shiho nage (pic. 5-10).

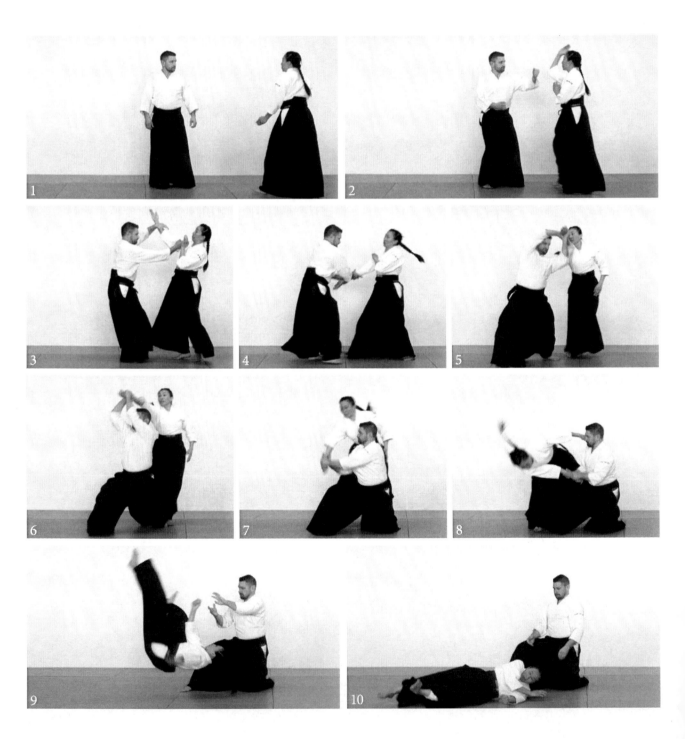

Tachi waza · yokomen uchi - irimi nage #1

Begin in left profile stance. As uke approaches and attacks, move slightly back to absorb and accelerate the attack (pic. 1-3). As uke gets closer, use your left forearm to apply atemi and open uke's right arm. Step forward and with your right hand enter onto uke's center line and execute irimi nage (pic. 4-8).

Tachi waza · yokomen uchi - irimi nage #2

Begin in left profile stance. As uke approaches and attacks, step back and with your right hand apply atemi (pic. 1-2). Deflect uke's yokomen uchi attack while stepping back (pic. 3-5). Step forward, use your forearm to close uke's center line, and finish irimi nage (pic. 6-9).

Tachi waza · yokomen uchi - irimi nage #3

Begin in left profile stance. As uke approaches and attacks, move sideways. With your left hand apply atemi onto uke's center line and open uke's right arm. With your right hand apply second atemi (pic. 1-3). Use your right forearm to lift uke's right arm and with your left hand apply atemi into uke's ribs (pic. 4-5). With your right hand, bring down uke's right arm and with your left hand, take control of uke's neck. Use your right forearm to close uke's center line and execute irimi nage (pic. 6-9).

Tachi waza · yokomen uchi - yoko irimi

Begin in left profile stance. As uke approaches and attacks, shift back and turn away (pic. 1-4). Once uke gets closer, turn and shift toward uke, unfold your left arm onto uke's center line, and execute yoko irimi (pic. 5-8).

Tachi waza · yokomen uchi - sumi otoshi

Begin in right profile stance. As uke approaches and attacks, use your right hand to apply atemi onto uke's center line. Move sideways and open uke's left arm (pic. 1-3). With your left hand, enter into uke's elbow pit, step forward, and finish sumi otoshi (pic. 4-8).

Tachi waza · yokomen uchi - tai otoshi

Begin in left profile stance. As uke approaches and attacks, use your left hand to apply atemi onto uke's center line. Move slightly sideways and begin to pivot while rotating your left forearm around uke's right arm (pic. 1-5). As uke comes around, take over uke's wrist and use your right hand to apply atemi. Step forward. Enter under uke's right armpit, and finish tai otoshi (pic. 6-9).

Tachi waza · yokomen uchi - ude kime nage

Begin in left profile stance. As uke approaches and attacks, use your left hand to apply atemi. Step back and take control of uke's right wrist. With your right hand apply second atemi, then take over uke's wrist and pull it sideways (pic. 1-5). Step in. With your left arm enter under and against uke's right arm and execute ude kime nage (pic. 6-9).

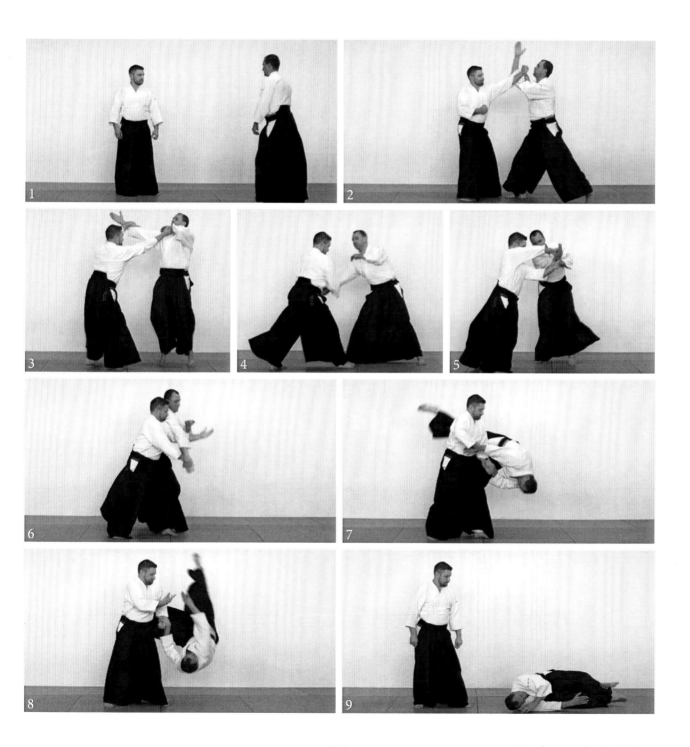

Tachi waza · yokomen uchi - koshi nage

Begin in left profile stance. As uke approaches and attacks, use your left hand to apply atemi. Step back, retract your left forearm, and control uke's right arm. Use your right hand to apply second atemi (pic. 1-3). Apply transitional ikkyo omote (pic. 4-6). Loosen up ikkyo hold so uke is able to rise. Swiftly half squat, load uke onto your hips, rise, and finish koshi nage (pic. 7-10).

Tachi waza · yokomen uchi - kaiten nage ura

Begin in left profile stance. As uke approaches and attacks, use your left hand to apply atemi onto uke's center line. Move sideways while rotating your left forearm around uke's right arm. Keep your forearm on uke's elbow and use your right hand to take control of uke's neck (pic. 1-5). Shift further back, pivot, and finish kaiten nage ura (pic. 6-10).

Tachi waza · yokomen uchi - kokyu nage

Begin in left profile stance. As uke approaches and attacks, use your left hand to apply atemi. Step back, retract your left hand, and hook it over uke's forearm. Use your right hand to apply the second atemi (pic. 1-3). With your right forearm swiftly cut into uke's elbow pit, turn into the direction of the throw, and finish kokyu nage (pic. 4-8).

Tsuki

Tachi waza · tsuki - ikkyo

Begin in left profile stance. As uke approaches and attacks, change your profile position. Use your left forearm to deflect uke's attack and your right hand to apply atemi (pic. 1-3). With your right hand take over uke's right wrist. With your left hand take control of uke's right elbow and finish ikkyo omote (pic. 4-8).

Tachi waza · tsuki - kotegaeshi

Begin in left profile stance. As uke approaches and attacks, move forward and off the line. With your left hand block uke's attack at uke's elbow pit and take over uke's wrist. With your right hand apply atemi (pic. 1-3). Pull uke into kuzushi and execute kotegaeshi (pic. 5-8).

Tachi waza · tsuki - kaiten nage

Begin in left profile stance. As uke approaches and attacks, move forward and off the line. With your left forearm suppress uke's attack at uke's elbow pit. With your right hand apply atemi and take over uke's neck (pic. 1-4). Pull uke's neck down, push uke's elbow forward, and finish kaiten nage (pic. 5-8).

Tachi waza · tsuki - ude kime nage

Begin in left profile stance. As uke approaches and attacks, move forward and off the line. With your left arm deflect the attack from outside. With your right hand apply atemi (pic. 1-3). Slide your right hand down and take control over uke's right wrist. With your left arm enter under and against uke's right arm. Step in and execute ude kime nage (pic. 4-7).

Tachi waza · tsuki - ude kime osae

Begin in left profile stance. As uke approaches and attacks, move forward and off the line. With your left hand deflect uke's attack and take over uke's right wrist. With your right hand apply atemi. With both hands take control of uke's right arm (pic. 1-4). Wrap your left arm over uke's right elbow (pic. 5). Simultaneously rotate sideways, descend into half seated position, and finish ude kime osae (pic. 6-8).

Tachi waza · tsuki - irimi nage

Begin in left profile stance. As uke approaches and attacks, move forward and off the line. With your left hand deflect uke's attack. Step forward, use your right hand to enter onto uke's center line, and finish irimi nage (pic. 1-5).

Tachi waza · tsuki - yoko irimi

Begin in left profile stance. As uke approaches and attacks, move forward and off the line. With your left hand deflect uke's attack (pic. 1-3). Immediately close uke's center line with your left elbow and execute yoko irimi (pic. 4-6).

Tachi waza · tsuki - sumi otoshi

Begin in left profile stance. As uke approaches and attacks, move forward and off the line. Use your left hand to block uke's attack and your right hand to apply atemi. Take over uke's wrist and pivot (pic. 1-4). As uke comes around, use your right hand to apply atemi and enter into uke's elbow pit, and finish sumi otoshi (pic. 5-8).

Mae Geri

Tachi waza · mae geri - kaiten nage

Begin in left profile stance. As uke attacks, move forward and enter on the inner side. With your left arm deflect and scoop uke's right leg. With your right hand, apply atemi and take over uke's neck (pic. 1-4). Step back and simultaneously pull uke's neck forward and down. Push uke's right leg up and forward and finish kaiten nage (pic. 5-8).

Tachi waza · mae geri - irimi nage

Begin in left profile stance. As uke attacks, shift sideways. Use your right forearm to deflect uke's attack and your left arm to block uke's right arm to prevent the possibility of tsuki attack (pic. 1-5). Step forward. With your right hand close uke's center line and finish irimi nage (pic. 6-8).

Tachi waza · mae geri - irimi nage #2

Begin in right profile stance. As uke attacks, simultaneously move forward and enter on the inner side. With your left arm deflect and scoop uke's right leg. With your right hand enter onto uke's center line and execute irimi nage (pic. 1-6).

Tachi waza · mae geri - irimi nage #3

Begin in left profile stance. As uke attacks, simultaneously move forward and enter on the inner side. Use your left arm to deflect and scoop uke's right leg and your right hand to control uke's center line (pic. 1-4). Simultaneously lift uke's right leg, sweep uke's left leg with your right, enter onto uke's center line with your right hand, and execute irimi nage (pic. 5-8).

Tachi waza · mae geri - yoko irimi

Begin in left profile stance. As uke attacks, simultaneously move forward and shift sideways. With your right forearm deflect uke's attack. With your left arm block uke's right arm to prevent the possibility of tsuki attack (pic. 1-3). As uke passes by, use your left elbow to enter onto uke's center line. Unfold your arm and execute yoko irimi (pic. 4-8).

Tachi waza · mae geri - lift throw

Begin in left profile stance. As uke attacks, simultaneously move forward and shift sideways. Use your right arm to deflect and scoop uke's right leg and your left hand to take control of uke's lower back (pic. 1-4). Lift uke off the ground, continue the forward motion, and let uke go (pic. 5-8).

Tachi waza · mae geri - pull throw

Begin in left profile stance. As uke attacks, move forward and shift sideways. Use your right arm to deflect and scoop uke's right leg. Use your left hand to take control of uke's right knee (pic. 1-4). simultaneously use your right arm to pull uke's leg up and your left hand to push uke's knee down and pull uke forward (pic. 5-9).

Tachi waza · mae geri - yonkyo

Begin in right profile stance. As uke attacks, simultaneously move forward and enter on the inner side. With your left arm deflect and scoop uke's right leg. With your right hand apply atemi and take over uke's right knee (pic. 1-5). Turn uke's knee inward, so that uke turns face down. Pull uke back and finish yonkyo (pic. 6-8).

Tachi waza · mae geri - kotegaeshi

Begin in left profile stance. As uke attacks, simultaneously move forward and shift sideways. With your right forearm deflect uke's attack (pic. 1-4). As uke attacks with tsuki jodan, use your left hand to deflect the attack and take over uke's wrist. Pull uke into kuzushi and execute kotegaeshi (pic. 5-10).

Ushiro Ryote Dori

Tachi waza · ushiro ryote dori - ikkyo omote

Offer your right hand for uke to grab. As uke connects, simultaneously pull uke sideways and behind (pic. 1-3). Once uke comes around, offer your left hand for uke to catch. Just before uke is able to catch it, remove your hand in a downward circular motion, take over uke's right elbow, and finish ikkyo omote in seiza (pic. 4-8).

Tachi waza · ushiro ryote dori - nikyo ura

Offer your right hand for uke to grab. As uke connects, simultaneously pull uke sideways and behind. Once uke comes around, offer your left hand for uke to catch. Just before uke is able to catch it, remove your hand in a downward circular motion and take over uke's right wrist (pic. 1-6). Set up nikyo ura hold and execute the technique (pic. 7-9). Apply nikyo vise and nikyo pin (pic. 10-12).

Tachi waza · ushiro ryote dori - sankyo omote

Offer your right hand for uke to grab. As uke connects, simultaneously pull uke sideways and behind. Once uke comes around, use your left hand to take over uke's right wrist and apply sankyo hold (pic. 1-4). Step back and off the line and execute sankyo omote (pic. 5-8).

Tachi waza · ushiro ryote dori - kotegaeshi

Offer your right hand for uke to grab. As uke connects, simultaneously pull uke sideways and behind. Once uke comes around, offer your left hand with the palm up (pic. 1-3). As uke catches your left wrist, step back, pivot, and use your right hand to take over uke's left wrist (pic. 4-5). Pull uke into kuzushi and execute kotegaeshi (pic. 7-9).

Tachi waza · ushiro ryote dori - shiho nage

Offer your right hand for uke to grab. As uke connects, simultaneously pull uke sideways and behind. Once uke comes around, offer your left hand with the palm up. As uke catches it, use your left hand to take over uke's left wrist and pull it around in a circular horizontal trajectory (pic. 1-5). Add your right hand to the hold, lock uke's arm, bring uke behind, and execute shiho nage (pic. 6-9).

Tachi waza · ushiro ryote dori - irimi nage

Offer your left hand for uke to grab. As uke connects, simultaneously pull uke sideways and behind. Once uke comes around, offer your right hand with the palm up (pic. 1-4). Once uke catches your right wrist, pull it back and change direction of uke's movement (pic. 5). Use your right forearm to close uke's center line and finish irimi nage (pic. 6-9).

Explore Aikido Vol. 1

Tachi waza · ushiro ryote dori - yoko irimi

Offer your right hand for uke to grab. As uke connects, pull uke sideways and behind. Once uke comes around, offer your left hand (pic. 1-4). As uke catches your left wrist, pivot. With meguri release your right hand from uke's grip. With your left arm pull uke forward (pic. 5). With your right forearm close uke's center line and execute yoko irimi (pic. 6-9).

Tachi waza · ushiro ryote dori - ude kime nage

Offer your left hand for uke to grab. As uke connects, simultaneously pull uke sideways and behind. Once uke comes around, offer your right hand with the palm up. As uke catches it, use your right hand to take over uke's right wrist and pull it around in a circular horizontal trajectory (pic. 1-5). Stretch uke's right arm sideways, use your left arm to enter under and against uke's right arm, and finish ude kime nage (pic. 7-9).

Tachi waza · ushiro ryote dori - koshi nage

Offer your right hand for uke to grab. As uke connects, simultaneously pull uke sideways and behind. Once uke is behind, offer your left hand (pic. 1-4). Before uke comes around, half squat and load uke onto your hips (pic. 5-6). Rise and finish koshi nage (pic. 7-9).

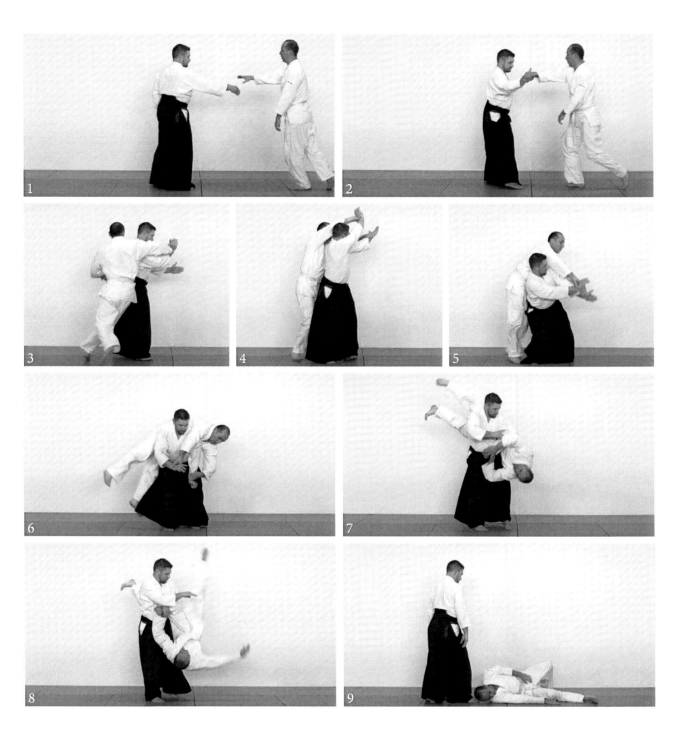

Tachi waza · ushiro ryote dori - juji garami

Offer your right hand for uke to grab. As uke connects, simultaneously pull uke sideways and behind. Once uke comes around, offer your left hand with the thumb up (pic. 1-4). As uke catches your left wrist, use your left hand to take over uke's left wrist and your right hand to take over uke's right wrist (pic. 5). Wrap uke's left arm over the right and execute juji garami (pic. 6-9).

Tachi waza · ushiro ryote dori - kaiten nage

Offer your left hand for uke to grab. As uke connects, simultaneously pull uke sideways and behind. Once uke comes around, offer your right hand (pic. 1-3). Before uke is able to catch it, escape with your right forearm in a circular motion and connect with uke's left elbow (pic. 4). Pivot and, with your left hand, take over uke's neck and pull it down. Use your right hand to take control of uke's elbow pit. Push it forward and finish kaiten nage (pic. 5-9).

Tachi waza · ushiro ryote dori - aiki otoshi

Offer your left hand for uke to grab. As uke connects, simultaneously pull uke sideways and behind. Once uke comes around, offer your right hand (pic. 1-3). As uke is about to grab your right wrist, shift back, place uke into kuzushi, and take over uke's knees (pic. 4-5). Pull uke's knees forward and up and finish aiki otoshi (pic. 6-9).

Tachi waza · ushiro ryote dori - nikyo irimi

Offer your right hand for uke to grab. As uke connects, simultaneously pull uke sideways and behind. Once uke comes around, offer your left hand (pic. 1-4). Escape with your left hand and let uke come forward. As uke passes by, use your right forearm to close uke's center line and finish nikyo irimi (pic. 5-9).

Tachi waza · ushiro ryote dori - kokyu nage

Offer your right hand for uke to grab. As uke connects, simultaneously pull uke sideways and behind. Once uke comes around, offer your left hand with the thumb up (pic. 1-4). As uke almost catches your left wrist, step forward and descend into half position. Pull uke forward and finish kokyu nage (pic. 5-9).

Katate Ushiro Kubi Shime, Ushiro Ryo Kata Dori & Ushiro Kubi Shime

Tachi waza · katate ushiro kubi shime - ikkyo omote

Offer your right hand for uke to grab. As uke connects, simultaneously pull uke sideways and behind. Once behind, uke attempts to apply left arm choke hold (pic. 1-3). Lift your right arm and move uke forward. With your left hand take over uke's right elbow and finish ikkyo omote (pic. 4-8).

Tachi waza · katate ushiro kubi shime - sankyo omote

Offer your right hand for uke to grab. As uke connects, simultaneously pull uke sideways and behind. Once behind, uke attempts to apply left arm choke hold (pic. 1-3). Lift your right arm and with your left hand take over uke's right wrist. Step in and execute sankyo omote (pic. 4-8).

Tachi waza · katate ushiro kubi shime - shiho nage sankyo

Offer your left hand for uke to grab. As uke connects, simultaneously pull uke sideways and behind. Once behind, uke attempts to apply right arm choke hold (pic. 1-4). Lift your left arm and with right forearm block uke's right elbow (pic. 5). Rotate sideways, turn uke with you, stretch uke's left arm, and finish shiho nage sankyo (pic. 6-7).

Tachi waza · katate ushiro kubi shime - koshi nage

Offer your right hand for uke to grab. As uke connects, simultaneously pull uke sideways and behind. Once behind, uke attempts to apply left arm choke hold (pic. 1-4). Stretch uke's right arm down and overlap it with your left forearm (pic. 6). Half squat, load uke onto your hips, rise, and finish koshi nage (pic. 7-10).

Tachi waza · katate ushiro kubi shime - kubi nage

Offer your right hand for uke to grab. As uke connects, simultaneously pull uke sideways and behind. Once behind, uke attempts to apply left arm choke hold (pic. 1-4). Stretch uke's right arm down (pic. 5-6). Wrap your left hand around uke's neck, add your right hand to the hold, and pull uke's neck down. Descend into seiza and finish kubi nage (pic. 7-10).

Tachi waza · katate ushiro kubi shime - kotegaeshi

Offer your left hand for uke to grab. As uke connects, simultaneously pull uke sideways and behind. Once behind, uke attempts to apply right arm choke hold (pic. 1-3). Lift your left arm and begin to pivot. Use your left hand to take over uke's right wrist, pull uke's grip off your gi, bring uke into kuzushi, and execute kotegaeshi (pic. 4-8).

Explore Aikido Vol. 1

Tachi waza · katate ushiro kubi shime - nikyo irimi

Offer your left hand for uke to grab. As uke connects, simultaneously pull uke sideways and behind. Once behind, uke attempts to apply right arm choke hold (pic. 1-3). Lift your left arm and turn toward uke (pic. 4). Let uke come closer and, once uke passes by, use your left forearm to close uke's center line, and execute nikyo irimi (pic. 4-8).

Tachi waza · katate ushiro kubi shime - yoko irimi

Offer your right hand for uke to grab. As uke connects, simultaneously pull uke sideways and behind. Once behind, uke attempts to apply left arm choke hold. At that moment lift your right arm and pivot (pic. 1-4). As you pivot, use meguri to release your right hand from uke's grip (pic. 5). Bring uke forward and execute yoko irimi (pic. 6-9).

Tachi waza · katate ushiro kubi shime - kokyu nage

Offer your left hand for uke to grab. As uke connects, simultaneously pull uke sideways and behind. Once behind, uke attempts to apply right arm choke hold (pic. 1-4). Lift your left arm while stepping forward. Descend into half position and finish kokyu nage (pic. 5-7).

Tachi waza · ushiro ryo kata dori - kokyu nage

Offer your right shoulder for uke to grab. As uke connects, use your right arm to push onto uke's arm and bring uke behind (pic. 1-3). Once behind, uke attempts to catch your left shoulder (pic. 4). Before uke is able to grab your shoulder, step forward and descend into half position. Lean forward and execute kokyu nage (pic. 5-7).

Tachi waza · ushiro ryo kata dori - aiki otoshi

Offer your left shoulder for uke to grab. As uke connects, use your left arm to push onto uke's arm and bring uke behind (pic. 1-3). Once behind, uke grabs your right shoulder. At that moment shift sideways and create space for uke to come around (pic. 4-5). As uke is next to you, half squat and take over uke's knees. Rise and pull uke's legs forward and up (pic. 6-10).

Tachi waza · ushiro ryo kata dori - yoko irimi

Offer your right shoulder for uke to grab. As uke connects, use your right arm to push onto uke's arm and bring uke behind (pic. 1-3). Once behind, uke grabs your left shoulder. At that moment pivot and step through and between uke's arms (pic. 4-6). Move forward and pull uke with you. As uke passes by, use your right arm to close uke's center line and execute yoko irimi (pic. 7-10).

Tachi waza · ushiro kubi shime - koshi nage

Offer your right shoulder for uke to grab. As uke connects, use your right arm to push onto uke's arm and bring uke behind (pic. 1-3). Once behind, uke wraps left arm around your neck and adds right hand to the choke hold. With both of your hands grab uke's left arm inside the elbow pit area and squat under uke's hips (pic. 4-7). Lean forward as in tachi rei, rise, and step back (pic. 8-10).

Futari Dori

Futari dori - kokyu nage #1

Begin in a profile position and offer your hands for ukes to grab (pic. 1-2). As ukes approach, and before they can apply a solid grip, move back swiftly. Descend into half position, incorporate elements of funakogi undo, pull ukes forward, and execute kokyu nage (pic. 3-8).

Futari dori - kokyu nage #2

Begin in a profile position and offer your hands for ukes to grab (pic. 1-2). As ukes approach, and before they can apply a solid grip, move back, fold your forearms, and bring both ukes up into kuzushi (pic. 3-5). Move forward, unfold your arms in a circular motion with meguri and finish kokyu nage (pic. 6-12).

Futari dori - sumi otoshi

Begin in a profile position and offer your hands for ukes to grab (pic. 1-2). As ukes approach and connect, use your right hand to take over first uke's left wrist and your left hand to take over second uke's left wrist. Pull ukes up into kuzushi (pic. 4-5). Throw each uke in opposite direction and finish sumi otoshi (pic. 6-10).

Futari dori - nikyo #1

Begin in a profile position and offer your hands for ukes to grab (pic. 1-2). As ukes approach, and before they can apply a solid grip, move back. Use your hands to encircle ukes wrists from inside out (pic. 3-5). Shift forward, push both grips toward both ukes centers, and finish nikyo (pic. 6-10).

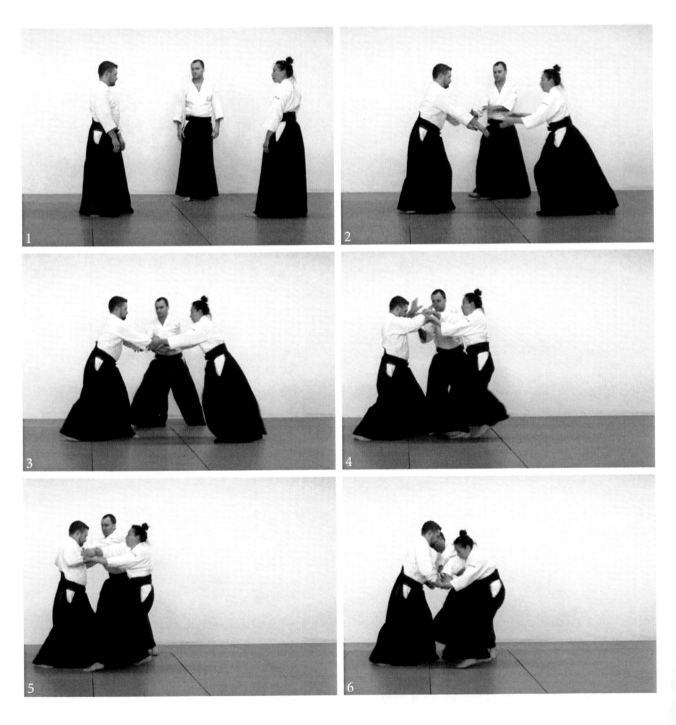

Futari dori - nikyo #2

Begin in a profile position and offer your hands for ukes to grab (pic. 1-2). As ukes approach, and before they can apply a solid grip, move back. Use your hands to encircle ukes wrists from outside in (pic. 3-6). Move back, bring your forearms toward your hips, and execute nikyo (pic. 7-12).

Futari dori - nikyo #3

Begin in a profile position and offer your hands for ukes to grab (pic. 1-2). As ukes approach, and before they can apply a solid grip, move back and encircle ukes wrists from inside out (pic. 3). Apply nikyo on first uke by bringing the hold toward your center and down. With a slight delay, execute nikyo on the second uke by pushing the grip sideways over the first uke (pic. 4-8).

Futari dori - nikyo #4

Begin in a profile position and offer your hands for ukes to grab (pic. 1-2). As ukes approach, and before they can apply a solid grip, move back and encircle first uke's wrist from inside out, and second uke's wrist from outside in (pic. 3). Simultaneously execute nikyo on both ukes: on first uke by pushing the grip downward toward uke's center, and on the second uke by pushing the grip behind (pic. 4-8).

Futari dori - yoko irimi

Move forward and offer your hands for ukes to grab (pic. 1-2). As ukes approach and connect, lift your right arm and walk under first uke's grip (pic. 3-4). Pull second uke forward and with first uke's arms close second uke's center line (pic. 5-6). Send both ukes sideways and finish yoko irimi (pic. 7-10).

Futari dori - irimi nage

Begin in a profile position and offer your hands for ukes to grab (pic. 1-2). As ukes are about to catch your forearms, shift back and pull back your arms to absorb and accelerate both ukes (pic. 3). Step forward, close both ukes center lines, and execute irimi nage (pic. 4-9).

Futari dori - shiho nage

Begin in a profile position and offer your hands for ukes to grab (pic. 1-2). As ukes approach, and before they can apply a solid grip, move back. Simultaneously take over both ukes' right wrists and pull them toward your center (pic. 3-5). Stretch ukes' arms outside, pass under them, and execute shiho nage (pic. 6-10).

Futari dori - sumi otoshi & nikyo

Begin in a profile position and offer your hands for ukes to grab (pic. 1-2). As ukes approach, and before they can apply a solid grip, move back. Take over first uke's right wrist and pull it up. Wrap your left hand around second uke's left wrist to set up nikyo (pic. 3). Execute both techniques simultaneously: sumi otoshi on first uke and nikyo on second uke (pic. 4-9).

Futari dori - nikyo irimi & irimi nage

Begin in a profile position and offer your hands for ukes to grab (pic. 1-2). As ukes approach, and before they can apply a solid grip, move back. Pull first uke up but don't let second uke grab your arm (pic. 3-4). Simultaneously execute nikyo irimi on first uke and direct irimi nage on second uke (pic. 5-9).

Explore Aikido Vol. 1

Futari dori - ikkyo

Begin in a profile position and offer your hands for ukes to grab (pic. 1-2). As ukes approach and connect, bring your right forearm onto your center and pass under first uke's grip (pic. 3-5). Stretch both ukes over each other and finish ikkyo omote in seiza (pic. 6-10).

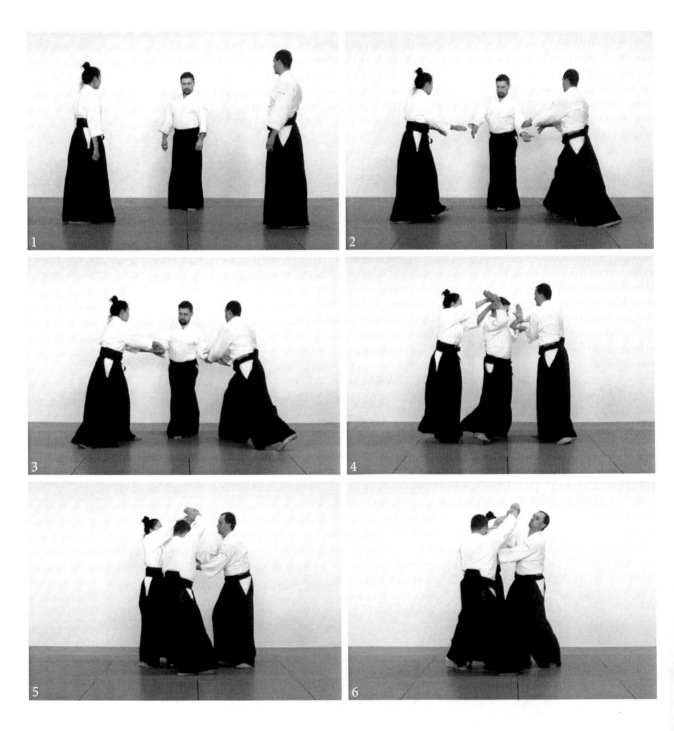

Explore Aikido Vol. 1

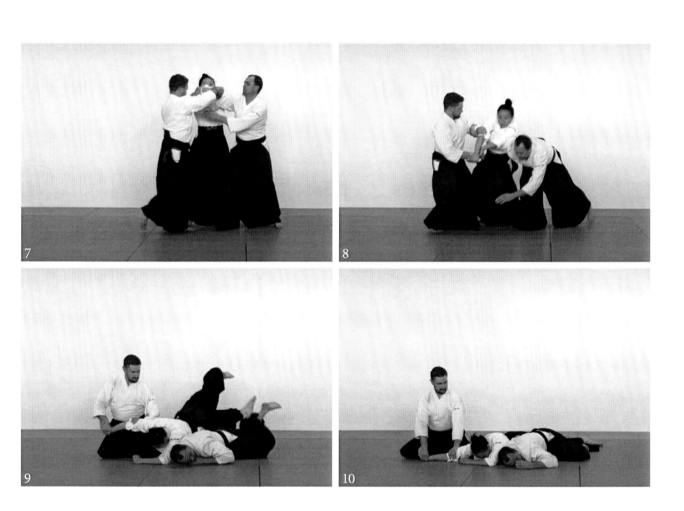

Randori

Randori within aikido repertoire is training against multiple attackers. This form of training is usually reserved for intermediate and advanced level aikidokas. Randori may vary from certain prearranged attacks to a more advanced level of training that incorporates variation of attacks (grips, strikes, kicks, etc.), as well as attack intensity by ukes, and technique execution by tori. During randori training tori has less time and space to execute techniques. Usually in randori, tori retreats to more direct techniques and atemi applications. With this being said, it is important to keep composure, execute techniques properly, and preserve the spirit of aikido. Remember that the most important aspects of training are safety and prevention of injury. Ability and skill level should be taken into consideration of all participants during randori session.

There are few guidelines to follow to make randori efficient:

1. Tori should end up outside of the circle. Meaning: if tori is surrounded by three ukes, at the moment of simultaneous approach/attack, tori should manage to exit the circle and leave all three ukes inside the circle's center.

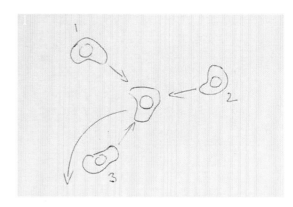

2. Use ukes as a shield. Meaning: once tori moves out of the circle center, tori should 'trade' position with one of the ukes and use that uke as a cover against the other two.

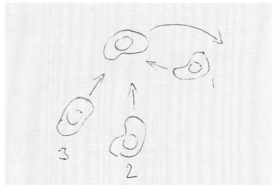

3. Use ukes against each other. Meaning: once tori is out of the circle and begins to apply techniques, he/she should throw ukes in the same direction and/or at each other.

Randori · example #1

This is a brief example of tachi waza randori. Tori begins in the center and three ukes are on the perimeter of the circle. As ukes start to attack, tori swiftly moves out of the center, trades places, and throws uke A onto uke B. This prevents uke B from attacking right away. It also increases distance between tori and uke C (pic. 1-3). As ukes A and B regain stability, tori executes irimi nage on uke C and simultaneously uses uke C as a cover against ukes A and B (pic. 4-8).

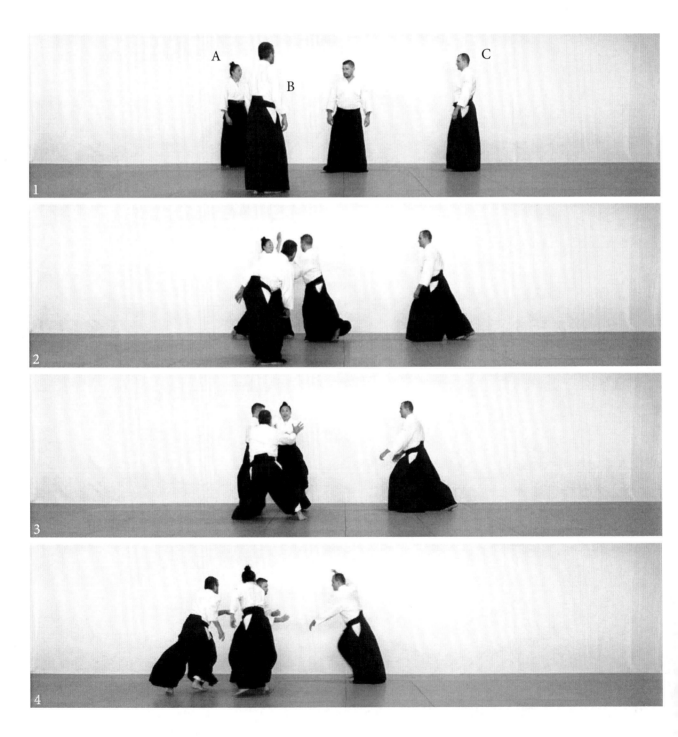

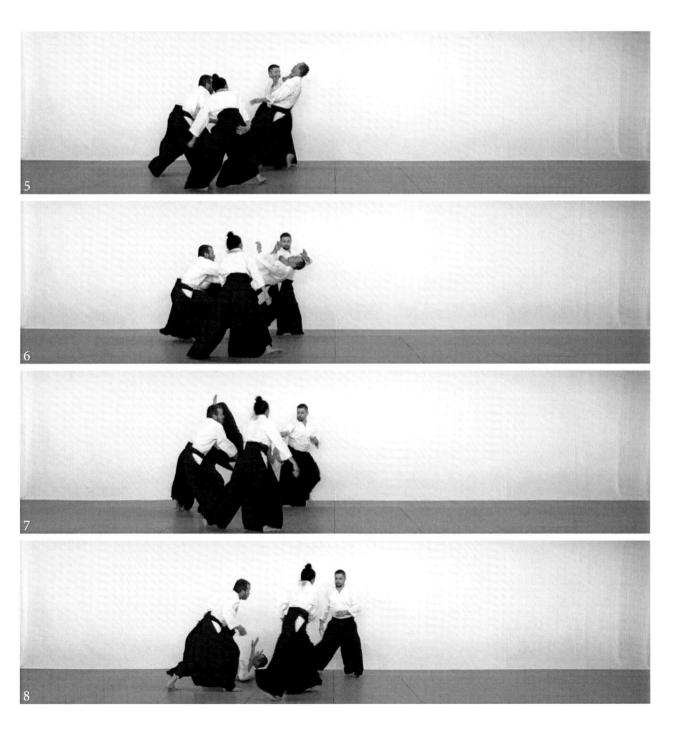

Randori · example #2

This is a quick example of hanmi handachi waza randori. Tori begins in the center and three ukes are on the perimeter of the circle. Tori swiftly moves out of the center, trades places, and throws uke C onto uke B (pic. 1-3). This prevents uke B from being able to attack right away. When uke A comes in, tori executes kokyu nage and ukes B and C follow. Tori continues with kokyu nage and then sudori nage, throwing all three ukes in one direction, onto each other (pic. 4-9).

Randori · example #3

One more example of tachi waza randori. This time, throwing ukes onto each other. Tori is in the center and three ukes are on the perimeter of the circle. As ukes start to attack, tori swiftly moves out of the center, trades places, and throws uke A onto uke B. This prevents uke B from being able to attack right away (pic. 1-4). Tori continues and throws uke C onto uke A & B (pic. 5-8).

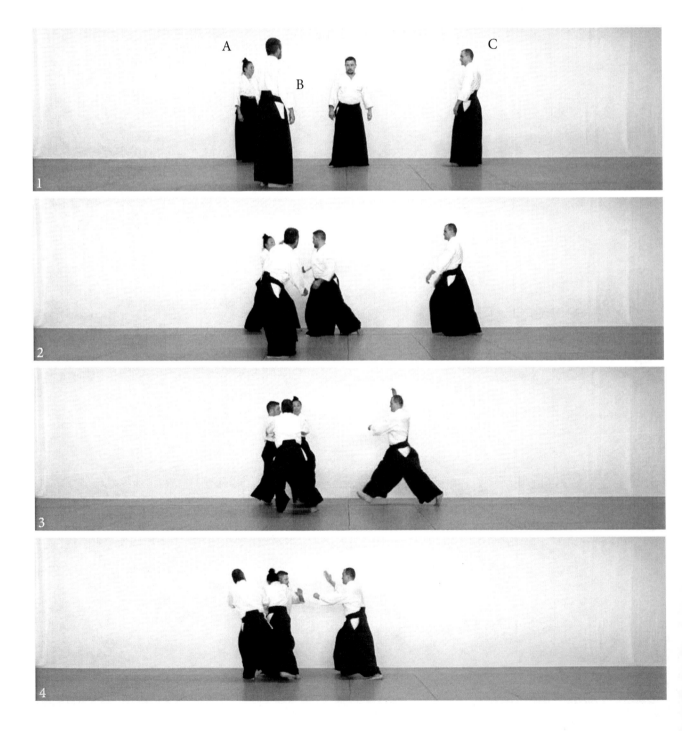

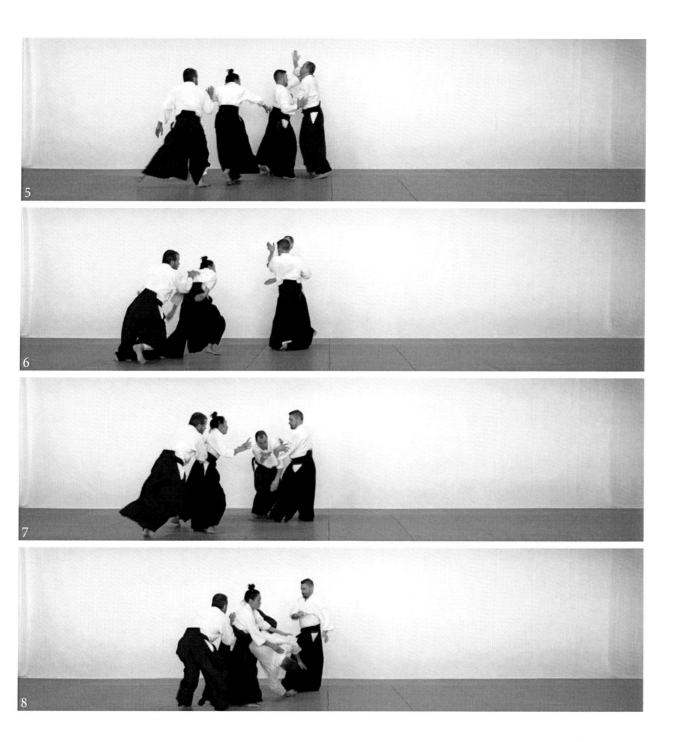

Kaeshi Waza

Kaeshi waza are counter techniques. In order to train kaeshi waza in a progressing manner, both uke and tori need to be familiar and technically skilled with at least the basic aikido techniques and concepts.

Kaeshi waza · ikkyo - ikkyo

Begin with left hand shomen uchi. Uke responds with ikkyo omote (pic. 1-2). Pivot and draw uke in a circular motion (pic. 3-5). As uke comes around, finish ikkyo omote in seiza (pic. 6-8).

Kaeshi waza · ikkyo - nikyo

Begin with right hand shomen uchi. Uke responds with ikkyo omote (pic. 1-2). Pivot and absorb uke in a circular motion (pic. 3-4). As uke comes around, finish nikyo ura (pic. 5-8).

Kaeshi waza · ikkyo - sankyo

Begin with right hand shomen uchi. Uke responds with ikkyo omote (pic. 1-2). Pivot and draw uke in a circular motion (pic. 3-4). As uke comes around, use your left hand to remove uke's left palm off your elbow. Use your right hand to regrab uke's left wrist and finish sankyo (pic. 5-8).

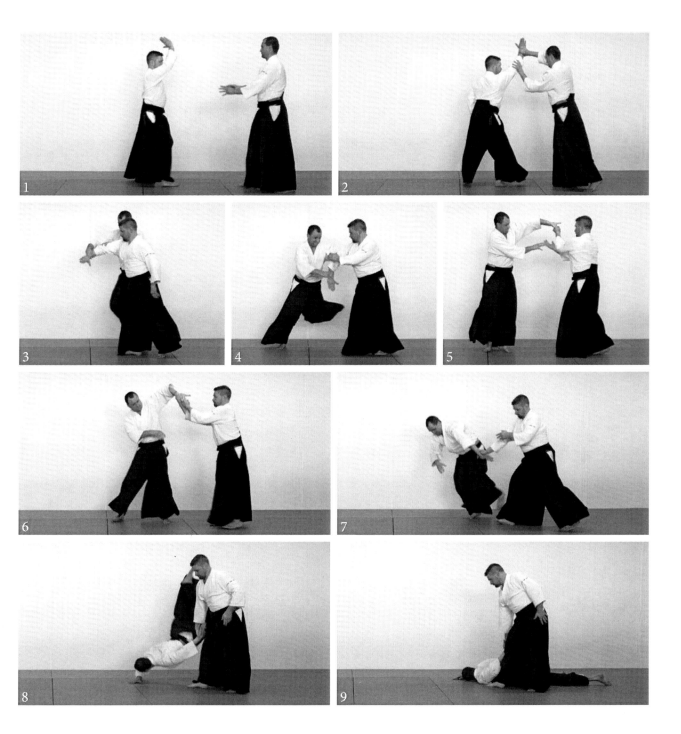

Kaeshi waza · ikkyo - kotegaeshi

Begin with left hand shomen uchi. Uke responds with ikkyo omote (pic. 1-2). Pivot and draw uke in a circular motion. As uke is about to come around, use your right hand to take over uke's left wrist. Pull uke's wrist forward (pic. 3-5). Once uke is in kuzushi, execute kotegaeshi (pic. 6-10).

Kaeshi waza · ikkyo - ude kime nage

Begin with left hand shomen uchi. Uke responds with ikkyo omote (pic. 1-2). Pivot and draw uke in a circular motion (pic. 3-4). As uke comes around, redirect uke to create opening under uke's left arm and execute ude kime nage (pic. 5-8).

Kaeshi waza · ikkyo - irimi nage

Begin with left hand shomen uchi. Uke responds with ikkyo omote (pic. 1-2). Pivot and absorb uke in a circular motion (pic. 3-4). As uke comes around, draw uke in and finish irimi nage (pic. 5-8).

Kaeshi waza · ikkyo - nikyo irimi

Begin with left hand shomen uchi. Uke responds with ikkyo omote (pic. 1-2). Pivot and absorb uke in a circular motion (pic. 3-4). As uke comes around, use meguri to draw uke in and up, and execute nikyo irimi (pic. 5-8).

Kaeshi waza · ikkyo - juji garami

Begin with right hand shomen uchi. Uke responds with ikkyo omote (pic. 1-2). Pivot and absorb uke in a circular motion (pic. 3-4). As uke comes around, use your left hand to scoop uke's left forearm off your right elbow. Take over uke's wrists and finish juji garami (pic. 5-9).

Kaeshi waza · ikkyo - shiho nage sankyo

Begin with left hand shomen uchi. Uke responds with ikkyo omote (pic. 1-2). Shift back and draw uke in (pic. 3-4). Once uke passes by, execute shiho nage sankyo (pic. 5-8).

Explore Aikido Vol. 1

Kaeshi waza · ikkyo - kokyu nage

Begin with left hand shomen uchi. Uke responds with ikkyo omote (pic. 1-2). Swiftly descend into half position and send uke forward into kokyu nage (pic. 3-8).

Kaeshi waza · nikyo ura - ikkyo

Begin with left hand shomen uchi. Uke responds with nikyo ura (pic. 1-3). Simultaneously flex your left forearm, pivot, and add meguri with your left forearm (pic. 3-6). Take over uke's left wrist and elbow and finish ikkyo omote in seiza (pic. 7-10).

Kaeshi waza · nikyo ura - nikyo

Begin with left hand shomen uchi. Uke responds with nikyo ura (pic. 1-3). Use your right hand to hold down uke's right palm and your left elbow to enter over uke's right forearm and execute nikyo (pic. 4-8).

Kaeshi waza · nikyo ura - sankyo

Begin with left hand shomen uchi. Uke responds with nikyo ura (pic. 1-3). Simultaneously flex your left forearm, pivot, and add meguri with your left forearm (pic. 4-5). Use your right hand to take over uke's left wrist and finish sankyo omote (pic. 6-10).

Kaeshi waza · nikyo ura - kotegaeshi

Begin with left hand shomen uchi. Uke responds with nikyo ura (pic. 1-3). With your left hand from the top, encircle uke's right forearm and take over uke's wrist (pic. 4-5). Pull uke into kuzushi and execute kotegaeshi (pic. 6-10).

Kaeshi waza · nikyo ura - nikyo irimi

Begin with right hand shomen uchi. Uke responds with nikyo ura (pic. 1-3). Simultaneously step back and draw uke in (pic. 4-5). As uke passes by, close uke's center line and execute nikyo irimi (pic. 6-9).

Kaeshi waza · nikyo ura - yoko irimi

Begin with left hand shomen uchi. Uke responds with nikyo ura (pic. 1-3). With your left hand pass between uke's arms and through uke's center line. With meguri scoop uke's right forearm (pic. 3-5). Draw uke in and finish yoko irimi (pic. 6-9).

Kaeshi waza · nikyo ura - shiho nage

Begin with left hand shomen uchi. Uke responds with nikyo ura (pic. 1-3). With your left hand pass between uke's arms and through uke's center line. With meguri scoop uke's right forearm. With both hands take control of uke's right forearm and execute shiho nage (pic. 4-9).

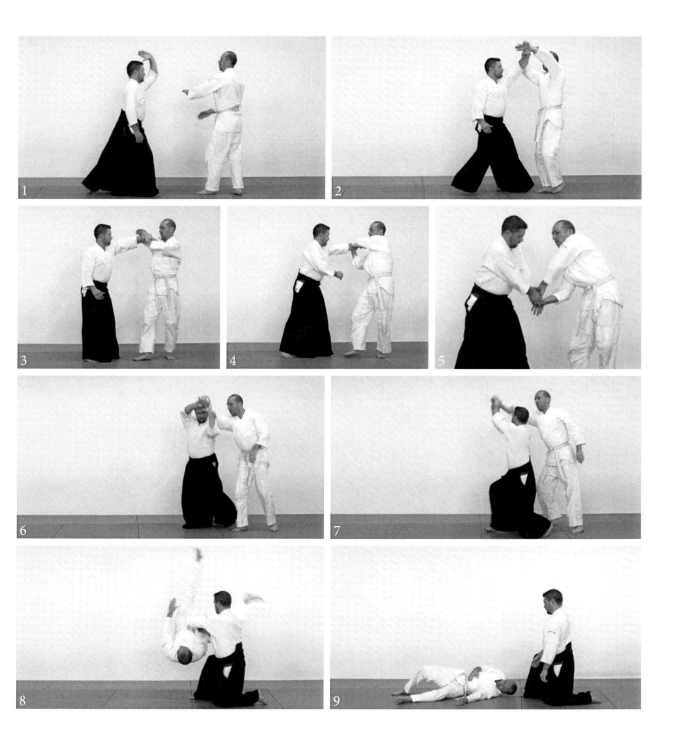

Kaeshi waza · nikyo ura - juji garami

Begin with left hand shomen uchi. Uke responds with nikyo ura (pic. 1-3). Simultaneously flex your left forearm, pivot, and add meguri with your left forearm (pic. 4-6). With your left hand take over uke's left wrist. With your right hand take over uke's right wrist and execute juji garami (pic. 7-11).

Kaeshi waza · nikyo ura - koshi nage

Begin with left hand shomen uchi. Uke responds with nikyo ura (pic. 1-3). With your left hand pass between uke's arms and through uke's center line. With meguri scoop uke's right forearm and take temporary control of uke's right forearm with both hands (pic. 3-4). Continue with right hand hold only and bring uke up and forward. Half squat, load uke onto your hips, and execute koshi nage (pic. 5-8).

Kaeshi waza · nikyo ura - ude kime nage

Begin with left hand shomen uchi. Uke responds with nikyo ura (pic. 1-3). With your left hand pass between uke's arms and through uke's center line. With meguri scoop uke's right forearm. With your right hand take over uke's right wrist (pic. 4-5). Stretch uke's right arm sideways and execute ude kime nage (pic. 6-10).

Kaeshi waza · nikyo ura - kokyu nage

Begin with left hand shomen uchi. Uke responds with nikyo ura (pic. 1-3). With your left hand pass between uke's arms and through uke's center line. Exit on the front side of uke and finish kokyu nage in a circular motion (pic. 4-9).

Kaeshi waza · sankyo - sankyo

Begin with left hand shomen uchi. Uke responds with sankyo (pic. 1-3). With your left hand, begin meguri and draw uke forward (pic. 4-6). With your right hand, take over uke's wrist and finish sankyo omote (pic. 7-10).

Kaeshi waza · sankyo - yoko irimi

Begin with left hand shomen uchi. Uke responds with sankyo (pic. 1-3). With your left hand pass between uke's arms and through uke's center line. With meguri scoop uke's right forearm, draw uke in, and finish yoko irimi (pic. 4-8).

Kaeshi waza · sankyo - shiho nage sankyo irimi

Begin with left hand shomen uchi. Uke responds with sankyo (pic. 1-3). Turn your hips away and absorb uke forward (pic. 4). As uke passes by, execute shiho nage sankyo irimi (pic. 5-9).

Kaeshi waza · sankyo - kokyu nage

Begin with right hand shomen uchi. Uke responds with sankyo (pic. 1-3). Step back. With your right forearm meguri bring uke in and finish kokyu nage (pic. 4-9).

Kaeshi waza · kotegaeshi - shiho nage

Begin with left hand shomen uchi. Uke responds with kotegaeshi (pic. 1-2). With your left hand from the top, encircle uke's right forearm. Use both hands to take over uke's wrist (pic. 3-5). Through an arm lock bring uke behind and around, and finish shiho nage (pic. 6-9).

Kaeshi waza · kotegaeshi - yoko irimi

Begin with left hand shomen uchi. Uke responds with kotegaeshi (pic. 1-3). With your left hand pass over uke's right arm and through uke's center line. With meguri scoop uke's right forearm, bring uke forward, and finish yoko irimi (pic. 4-8).

Kaeshi waza · kotegaeshi - ude kime nage

Begin with right hand shomen uchi. Uke responds with kotegaeshi (pic. 1-2). Step back and absorb uke with right hand meguri (pic. 3-5). With your left arm enter under and against uke's arms and execute ude kime nage (pic. 6-9).

Kaeshi waza · kotegaeshi - koshi nage

Begin with left hand shomen uchi. Uke responds with kotegaeshi (pic. 1-3). Step forward, bring your elbow inward onto your center line, and bring uke in with you (pic. 4-5). Stretch uke up and forward. Half squat, load uke onto your hips, and execute koshi nage (pic. 6-9).

Kaeshi waza · kotegaeshi - sumi otoshi

Begin with right hand shomen uchi. Uke responds with kotegaeshi (pic. 1-2). With your right hand in a circular motion, take over uke's left wrist into sankyo hold (pic. 3-6). Bring uke forward and finish sumi otoshi (pic. 7-10).

Kaeshi waza · kotegaeshi - nikyo irimi

Begin with right hand shomen uchi. Uke responds with kotegaeshi (pic. 1-3). Step back and draw uke in with right hand meguri (pic. 3-5). As uke passes by, close uke's center line and execute nikyo irimi (pic. 6-9).

Kaeshi waza · kotegaeshi - kokyu nage

Begin with left hand shomen uchi. Uke responds with kotegaeshi (pic. 1-3). Step forward, bring your elbow inward onto your center line, and bring uke in with you (pic. 4-5). Unfold your left arm and finish kokyu nage (pic. 6-8).

Kaeshi waza · shiho nage - shiho nage

Begin with left hand katate tori aihanmi. Uke responds with shiho nage (pic. 1-2). Pivot and pull uke in with you (pic. 3-4). As uke comes around, use the momentum, bring uke behind you and finish shiho nage (pic. 5-9).

Kaeshi waza · shiho nage - ude kime nage

Begin with left hand katate tori aihanmi. Uke responds with shiho nage (pic. 1-2). Pivot and pull uke in with you (pic. 3-4). As uke comes around, stretch uke's arm sideways and finish ude kime nage (pic. 5-9).

Kaeshi waza · shiho nage - irimi nage

Begin with left hand katate tori aihanmi. Uke responds with shiho nage (pic. 1-4). As uke is about to finish shiho nage, relax your arm, step back, bring uke forward, and execute irimi nage (pic. 5-8).

Kaeshi waza · shiho nage - yoko irimi

Begin with left hand katate tori aihanmi. Uke responds with shiho nage (pic. 1-3). Turn your hips away and use your left arm to bring uke forward (pic. 4). As uke passes by, finish yoko irmi (pic. 5-8).

Kaeshi waza · shiho nage - sumi otoshi

Begin with left hand katate tori aihanmi. Uke responds with shiho nage (pic. 1-3). As uke begins shiho nage, turn your hips away. Use your left hand to take over uke's left wrist, pull uke up, and execute sumi otoshi (pic. 4-9).

Kaeshi waza · ude kime nage - yoko irimi

Begin with left hand katate tori aihanmi. Uke responds with ude kime nage (pic. 1-3). Pivot and bring uke with you (pic. 4). As uke comes around, use your left hand to pull uke forward, close uke's center line with your right arm, and finish yoko irimi (pic. 5-8).

Kaeshi waza · ude kime nage - irimi nage

Begin with left hand katate tori aihanmi. Uke responds with ude kime nage (pic. 1-3). Pivot and bring uke with you (pic. 4). As uke comes around, use your left hand to pull uke forward. As uke passes by, finish irimi nage (pic. 5-9).

Kaeshi waza · ude kime nage - shiho nage

Begin with left hand katate tori aihanmi. Uke responds with ude kime nage (pic. 1-3). Pivot and bring uke with you (pic. 4-5). As uke comes around, add your right hand grip to uke's left wrist, and finish shiho nage (pic. 6-10).

Kaeshi waza · ude kime nage - kotegaeshi

Begin with left hand katate tori aihanmi. Uke responds with ude kime nage (pic. 1-3). Pivot and bring uke with you (pic. 4). Use your right hand to take over uke's right wrist. Pull uke forward into kuzushi and execute kotegaeshi (pic. 5-9).

Kaeshi waza · ude kime nage - ude kime nage

Begin with left hand katate tori aihanmi. Uke responds with ude kime nage (pic. 1-3). As uke comes around, stretch uke's arm sideways. Use your right hand to take control of uke's left elbow and finish ude kime nage (pic. 4-8).

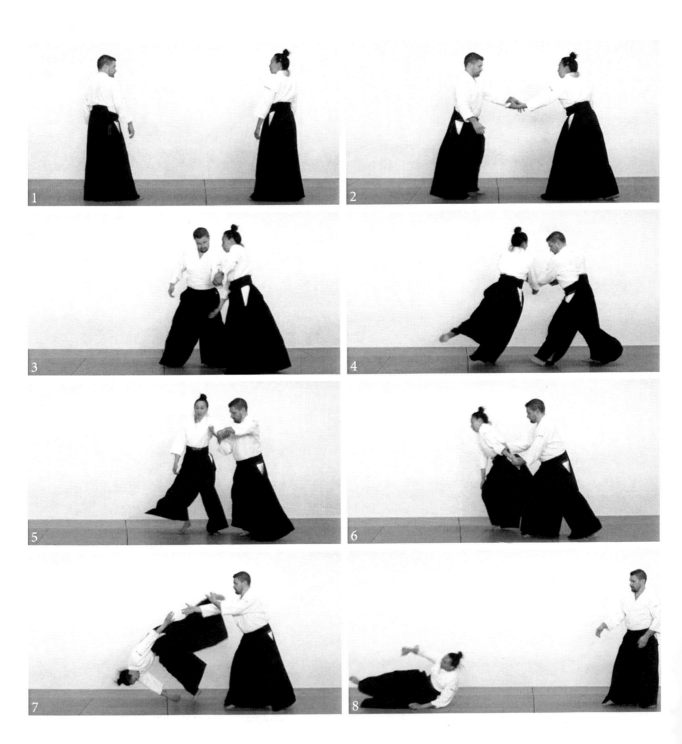

Kaeshi waza · yoko irimi - yoko irimi

Begin with left hand katate tori gyakuhanmi. Uke responds with yoko irimi (pic. 1-3). Follow in, lift uke's right arm, step behind uke, and execute yoko irimi (pic. 4-8).

Kaeshi waza · yoko irimi - yoko irimi #2

Begin with right hand katate tori gyakuhanmi. Uke responds with yoko irimi (pic. 1-2). Follow in. With your left hand control uke's left elbow and pivot under uke's left arm (pic. 3-5). With your left hand stretch uke forward and execute yoko irimi (pic. 6-8).

Kaeshi waza · yoko irimi - shiho nage

Begin with left hand katate tori gyakuhanmi. Uke responds with yoko irimi (pic. 1-3). Follow in. Lift uke's right arm and open uke's center line with a circular motion. With your right hand apply atemi (pic. 4-5). With both hands take over uke's right wrist and execute shiho nage (pic. 6-10).

Kaeshi waza · yoko irimi - sumi otoshi

Begin with right hand katate tori gyakuhanmi. Uke responds with yoko irimi (pic. 1-3). Follow in. Lift uke's left arm and open uke's center line with a circular motion. Use your left hand to apply atemi and slide it into uke's elbow pit (pic. 4-6). Step forward and finish sumi otoshi (pic. 7-9).

Kaeshi waza · yoko irimi - kubi nage

Begin with right hand katate tori gyakuhanmi. Uke responds with yoko irimi (pic. 1-2). Follow in. Use your left hand to take control of uke's left elbow and move forward under uke's left arm (pic. 3-4). Wrap your left arm around uke's neck, add your right arm to the hold, and finish kubi nage (pic. 5-9).

Explore Aikido Vol. 1

Japanese - English Glossary

Ai - harmony
aiki-jo - aikido training with wooden staff
aiki-ken - aikido training with wooden sword
arigato - thanks, thank you
ashi - foot, leg
ashikubi - ankle
atemi - strike, blow
ayumi ashi - regular step, ordinary walking, where the legs move forward alternately

Bokken - wooden sword
budo - Japanese martial arts
bushi - warrior
bushido - feudal-military Japanese code of behavior followed by the samurai

Chikama - shortest distance, face to face with the opponent
chudan - middle position

Dan - black belt rank
deshi - student
do - way, path
dojo - martial arts studio
dojo cho - chief instructor
domo arigato gozaimashita - thank you very much (used after each class to your partner and sensei)
dori - grab, hold

Futari Dori - training against two opponents

Geri - kick
gedan - lower position
godan - 5th degree black belt rank
gyakuhanmi - opposite stance, mirrored stance

Ha - edge of bokken's blade
hachidan - 8th degree black belt rank
hai - yes
hakama - traditional Japanese pants usually worn by black belt ranks or senior students
hara - abdomen
hanmi handachi waza - aikido practice in a seated position against standing attacker(s)
hidari - left
hiji - elbow
hiza - knee

Irimi - entering movement
irimi nage - entering throw, one of the fundamental aikido techniques

Jo - wooden staff
jo dori - techniques against uke equipped/attacking with jo.
jo omote - take your jo
jo ite - place your jo away
jodan - upper position
judan - 10th degree black belt rank

Kaeshi waza - counter techniques
kai - organization
kamae - position, stance
kamiza - an alter, place of honor. In the dojo it refers to a place where the portrait(s) of the school predecessor(s) and/or calligraphy scroll is displayed
kashira - back end of bokken's handle
keiko - training
ken dori - techniques for disarming an opponent equipped with bokken
ki - mind, spirit, energy
kihon - basic form
kensaki - tip of the bokken's blade
kokoro - heart, spirit
kokyuho - way or method of breathing
kokyu nage - "breath throw" techniques
kote - wrist
kotegaeshi - outward wrist turn or twist
kubi - neck
kuzushi - off balance position/unbalancing the opponent
kyu - any rank below black belt
kyudan - 9th degree black belt rank

Ma-ai - correct, proper distance
mae - front
meguri - flexibility and rotation of the forearms
men - face
mokuso - meditation
mono uchi - 6-8 inches of the blade closest to the sword's / bokken's tip
mune - 1) chest; 2) back of the bokken's blade
mushin - lit. no mind

Nage - throw
nanadan - 7th degree black belt rank
nanakyo - seventh pin
nidan - 2nd degree black belt rank
Nippon - Japan

O - grand, big
O'Sensei - grand master, in aikido this title refers to the founder of aikido, Morihei Ueshiba
obi - belt
omote - in the front direction (in aikido we can divide techniques into omote and ura)
onegai shimasu - in aikido training it is used at the beginning of each class and it can be understood as "please let me train with you"

Rei - bow
rokudan - 6th degree black belt rank
ryu - in budo it refers to school or style

Sandan - 3rd degree black belt rank
saya - scabbard
shiho nage - throw in four directions
seika tanden - central point of stomach located slightly below the navel
shikko - knee walking
seiza - kneeling seated position
seme - attacker, term especially used during aiki-ken and aiki-jo training. In aiki-tai jutsu the term would be replaced with "uke"
sensei - teacher, master, instructor
shite - defender, term especially used during aiki-ken and aiki-jo training. In aiki-tai jutsu the term is replaced with "tori"
shihan - master instructor
shinogi - bokken's blade ridge
shodan - 1st degree black belt rank
shomen - front or top of head
sode - sleeve
soto - outside, on the outside
suburi - basic jo or bokken practice in striking and thrusting
suwari waza - techniques in sitting position

Tachi waza - standing techniques
tai sabaki - body movements related to specific aikido techniques
tai jutsu - the art of the body (in aikido - unarmed techniques)
tachi rei - bow in standing position
tanto - knife. In aikido the term refers to wooden knife.
tatami - mat, padded flooring
te gatana - "hand sword"
tera - temple (body part)
toma - big distance
tori - the one who is carrying out the technique, the thrower. Also see "shite"
tsugi ashi - sliding and follow up step. Tsugi ashi vs. ayumi ashi
tsuba - bokken's hand guard
tsuka - bokken's handle
tsuki - punch

Uchi - open hand strike
uchi deshi - live-in student, direct student of the sensei
uke - attacker, person being thrown. Also see "seme"
ukemi waza - the art of falling in response to a technique
ura - rear
ushiro - behind, backward

Waza - technique, method, group of techniques

Yame - stop
yoko - side
yokomen - side of the head
yondan - 4th degree black belt rank
yudansha - any black belt rank holder

Zanshin - lit. remaining mind; alerted state of mind right after performing technique(s)
zarei - bow in a seiza
zori - sandals
zubon - pants

Japanese Counting

ichi - one
ni - two
san - three
shi/yon - four
go - five
roku - six
shichi/nana - seven
hachi - eight
kyu - nine
ju - ten

Other books of interest. Available from Amazon.com and other book stores.

Explore AIKIDO Vol. 2
Aiki-Jo
Staff Techniques in Aikido

The volume showcases a wide range of staff techniques in aikido including:

- Aiki-Jo Etiquette
- Jo Suburi
- Jo Kihon/Kata
- Jo Nage
- Jo Dori
- Kumi Jo

ISBN 13: 978-1948038010
ISBN 10: 1948038013

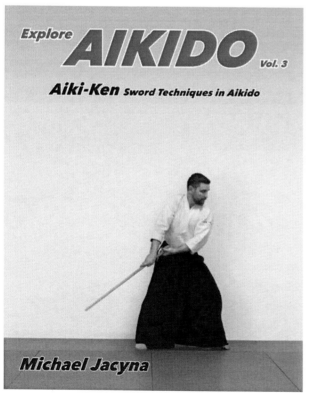

Explore AIKIDO Vol. 3
Aiki-Ken
Sword Techniques in Aikido

The volume showcases a wide range of sword techniques in aikido including:

- Aiki-Ken Etiquette
- Bokken Suburi
- Bokken Kihon/Kata
- Ken Nage
- Ken Dori
- Kumi Tachi

ISBN 13: 978-1948038027
ISBN 10: 1948038021

Made in United States
North Haven, CT
09 August 2023